Christian Friendship

Christian Friendship

Engaging the Tradition,
Transforming the Culture

JOHN P. BEQUETTE

CASCADE *Books* · Eugene, Oregon

CHRISTIAN FRIENDSHIP
Engaging the Tradition, Transforming the Culture

Cascade Books
An Imprint of Wipf and Stock Publishers
199 W. 8th Ave., Suite 3
Eugene, OR 97401

www.wipfandstock.com

PAPERBACK ISBN: 978-1-5326-5445-9
HARDCOVER ISBN: 978-1-5326-5446-6
EBOOK ISBN: 978-1-5326-5447-3

Cataloguing-in-Publication data:

Names: Bequette, John P., author.
Title: Christian friendship : engaging the tradition, transforming the culture / John P. Bequette.
Description: Eugene, OR : Cascade Books, 2019 | Includes bibliographical references.
Identifiers: ISBN 978-1-5326-5445-9 (paperback) | ISBN 978-1-5326-5446-6 (hardcover) | ISBN 978-1-5326-5447-3 (ebook)
Subjects: LCSH: Friendship—Religious aspects—Christianity.
Classification: BJ1533.F8 B46 2019 (print) | BJ1533.F8 B46 (ebook)

Manufactured in the U.S.A.   APRIL 22, 2019

I dedicate this book to my wife Nancy. She and I have learned—and continue to learn—the meaning of friendship through our conjugal life together.

Contents

Introduction

JOSEF PIEPER HAS ARGUED that leisure is the basis of culture. In his book by the same title, Pieper challenges the modern notion that work or productivity is the cause and guarantor of a vital human community. Behind the idolatry of work, he detects a "new conception of the meaning of human existence as such," specifically, that we do not work in order to live, but live in order to work.[1] Contrariwise, Pieper argues that leisure, which facilitates the Christian concept of the contemplative life, is the true basis for culture, for it allows the human person to realize his or her full humanity.[2] This full realization of what is essentially human is found in the liberal arts, which express genuine human freedom in that they are not subordinate to utility. Pieper writes: "The 'liberality' or 'freedom' of the liberal arts consists in their not being disposable for purposes, that they do not need to be legitimated by a social function, by being 'work.'"[3] Implicit in this is a specific understanding of culture as connected to a meaningful, fully realized human existence, at the heart of which is freedom.

While I believe that Pieper has identified the true basis of culture, we can go a step further. The fully realized human existence, which is the goal of culture, has a more specific character: relationality. The *Catechism of the Catholic Church* understands relationality as the defining feature of the human person created in the image of God:

1. Pieper, *Leisure*, 7, 4.
2. Pieper, *Leisure*, 5.
3. Pieper, *Leisure*, 22.

1

> Being in the image of God the human individual possesses the dignity of a person, who is not just something, but someone. He is capable of self-knowledge, of self-possession and of freely giving himself and entering into communion with other persons. And he is called by grace to a covenant with his Creator, to offer him a response of faith and love that no other creature can give in his stead.[4]

The human person's relational nature is expressed in his or her capacity for self-knowledge, self-possession, communion with others, and covenant with God. All of these capacities, of course, are interrelated. In order to enter into a relationship of communion with another person, I must in some real sense give myself to that person. Before I can do this, however, I must be in possession of myself. Self-possession makes relationship with others possible. The fact that I possess or own myself is the precondition for my ability to give myself to another person in a relationship. Moreover, self-possession entails self-knowledge. When I give myself to another, I have some sense of the self that I am giving. Ultimately, I am called to make this same self-donation to God in response to his prior self-donation to me. This responsive self-donation to the self-donation of God is the essence of covenant, which is fully expressed in the Paschal mystery, where God gives himself to the point of becoming one of us and giving his very life for us. This ability to enter into communion with others is at the heart of what it means to be a human person. A genuinely humane culture is one in which this is fully operative and expressed in laws, institutions, art, literature, education, economics, and family life.

But why is culture so important in the first place? Catholicism recognizes that culture is essential to what it means to be human. But what, exactly, *is* culture? The word "culture" derives from the Latin *cultus*, meaning "labor, care, or cultivation." An agrarian society cultivates its sustenance from the land. In a derivative sense, the Romans used the word "culture" to denote the care or cultivation of the person, which included education and

---

4. *Catechism of the Catholic Church*, para. 357.

refinement of manners. *Cultus* denoted a genuinely humane life distinguished from that of brute beasts. Cicero attributed this function to rhetoric, the art of speaking well, which in his view had the power to bring people together and civilize them: "What other power," he asks, "could have been strong enough either to gather scattered humanity into one place, or to lead it out of its brutish existence in the wilderness up to our present condition of civilization as men and as citizens [*ad hunc humanum cultum civilemque deducere*]?"[5] In this passage, the word *cultus* stands for the state of civilization, of living in organized human communities. *Cultus* or culture enables us to live in communion with others. Protestant church historian H. Richard Niebuhr understands culture to have three distinct characteristics. First, culture is social; it is "inextricably bound up with man's life in society."[6] Second, culture is a "human achievement."[7] It is "the work of men's minds and hands. It is that portion of man's heritage in any place or time which has been given us designedly and laboriously by other men."[8] It includes speech, education, traditions, stories and myths, art, science and technology, law, government, religion, and beliefs.[9] Third, culture is concerned with "the *temporal and material realization of values*" which are ordered to the good of human beings.[10] As a derivative of this third characteristic, cultural activity "is almost always as much concerned with the *conservation of values* as with their realization."[11] For our purposes, we can define culture as the collection of values, beliefs, and customs of a particular society or group, along with the artistic, intellectual, and social achievements derived therefrom. It is rooted in the shared values of a society or group of people and at the same time expresses these values. Furthermore, culture provides the material for further growth and

5. Cicero, *De Oratore*, 1.8.33.
6. Niebuhr, *Christ and Culture*, 32.
7. Niebuhr, *Christ and Culture*, 33.
8. Niebuhr, *Christ and Culture*, 33.
9. Niebuhr, *Christ and Culture*, 33.
10. Niebuhr, *Christ and Culture*, 35, 36, emphasis author's.
11. Niebuhr, *Christ and Culture*, 37, emphasis author's.

development in social life. Cultures can be considered "products of action" as well as "conditioning elements of further action."[12] Culture results from human interaction and provides the matrix for such action. We are social creatures, created for communion with others, and culture provides the wherewithal for this interpersonal communion. Culture is thus essential to the full realization of our vocation as human beings. While leisure makes the emergence of culture possible, I maintain that friendship is the apogee of culture, because friendship embodies human relationality in its purest and most noble form. Friendship is the crowning achievement of culture.

If my thesis is correct, then it follows that a healthy culture is one that nurtures friendship and enables it to thrive. By contrast, an unhealthy culture is one that hinders and finally destroys friendship. The ability to build meaningful friendships is essential to the full realization of our being made in the image of God. And if salvation consists in the restoration of this image in the person, then there is a salvific dimension to friendship and, consequently, a salvific dimension to culture. Peter Kreeft expresses this quite well in his defense of the "culture wars":

> I don't mean merely that Western civilization will die. That's a piece of trivia. I mean that eternal souls will die . . . That's what's at stake in this war: not just whether America will become a banana republic or whether we'll forget Shakespeare or even whether some nuclear terrorist will incinerate half of humanity, but whether our children and children's children will see God forever.[13]

Our eternal salvation depends, at least in part, on our ability to enter into meaningful friendships. This ability is intimately connected with culture. Thus, friendship is an issue that touches upon the salvation of souls and is therefore central to the mission of the church.

Contemporary culture, particularly in the West, is characterized by secularization. The values, beliefs, artistic and intellectual

12. Kroeber and Kluckhohn, *Culture*, 357; quoted in Lang, "Culture," 426.

13. Kreeft, *How to Win the Culture War*, 22.

4

achievements, and sociopolitical life express a widespread rejection of religious faith and of moral norms rooted in faith. Pope John Paul II recognized and critically analyzed this situation; indeed, it was one of the major themes of his pontificate. In his apostolic exhortation *Christifideles Laici*, John Paul pays particular attention to the fact that, in historically Christian countries, consumerism "inspires and sustains a life lived 'as if God did not exist.'"[14] What is worse, the faith exerts virtually no influence upon those events and occurrences in life where one is challenged to critically ponder the meaning of one's existence:

> Sometimes the Christian faith as well, while maintaining some of the externals of its tradition and rituals, tends to be separated from those moments of human existence which have the most significance, such as, birth, suffering, and death. In such cases, the questions and formidable enigmas posed by these situations, if remaining without responses, expose contemporary people to an inconsolable delusion or to the temptation of eliminating the truly humanizing dimension of life implicit in these problems.[15]

Key events in life call us to reflect upon the meaning of our existence. This is the "existential" dimension to John Paul II's thought: we discover the meaning of our lives in the concrete challenges and crises we encounter. Chief among these challenges is suffering. What could be the implicit "humanizing" dimension to suffering? In his apostolic letter *Salvifici Doloris*, John Paul writes that suffering "seems to be particularly essential to the nature of man."[16] He continues:

> It is as deep as man himself, precisely because it manifests in its own depth that which is proper to man, and in its own way surpasses it. Suffering seems to belong to man's transcendence: it is one of those points in which man is

---

14. John Paul II, *Christifideles Laici*, 3.34.
15. John Paul II, *Christifideles Laici*, 3.34.
16. John Paul II, *Salvifici Doloris*, 1.2.

in a certain sense "destined" to go beyond himself, and he is called to this in a mysterious way.[17]

The human person, created in God's image and likeness, has the capacity to go beyond the self, to transcend the limitations of individuality and connect with others. This is what we mean when we say that the human person is relational in nature. Suffering elicits interpersonal communion in that it evokes compassion and respect.[18] It elicits human relationality in its true depth. It is faith, moreover, that enables one to experience this transcendence in the midst of suffering. In the absence of a solid grounding in the faith, however, individuals are ill-equipped to face the anxieties and perplexities that are evoked during times of suffering and crisis. They then fall prey to the vacuous answers offered by a secular culture. Moreover, this alienation from a living faith has an even more sinister quality: it darkens our ability to perceive the presence of God in the world and the corresponding dignity of the human person created in God's image. In *Evangelium Vitae*, John Paul writes:

> We have to go to the heart of the tragedy being experienced by modern man: *the eclipse of the sense of God and of man*, typical of a social and cultural climate dominated by secularism, which, with its ubiquitous tentacles, succeeds at times in putting Christian communities themselves to the test.[19]

John Paul identifies a "sad vicious circle: *when the sense of God is lost, there is also a tendency to lose the sense of man*, of his dignity and his life."[20] What results from this is a "systematic violation of the moral law, especially in the serious matter of respect for human life and its dignity," which produces a "progressive darkening of the capacity to discern God's living and saving presence."[21] Secularization involves not merely the dechristianization of the culture;

17. John Paul II, *Salvifici Doloris*, 1.2.
18. John Paul II, *Salvifici Doloris*, 1.4.
19. John Paul II, *Evangelium Vitae*, 1.21, emphasis author's.
20. John Paul II, *Evangelium Vitae*, 1.21, emphasis author's.
21. John Paul II, *Evangelium Vitae*, 1.21.

it effects the dehumanization of human beings within that culture. For this reason, John Paul recognizes a vital connection between the proclamation of the gospel and the affirmation of the dignity of the human person: "The Gospel of God's love for man, the Gospel of the dignity of the person and the Gospel of life are a single and indivisible Gospel."[22] The gospel or "good news" of salvation in Jesus Christ contains the implicit good news of the dignity of the person.

In our current cultural climate, when our sense of God and man has become darkened, there is a need to make explicit the relationship between the gospel and human dignity. We see indications of this in the writings of Pope Benedict XVI and Pope Francis. Like John Paul, Benedict affirms a vital connection between the gospel and human dignity. To proclaim the gospel is to show the path toward human fulfillment, "to teach the art of living."[23] At the heart of this is the experience of interpersonal communion. Such communion begins with what Benedict calls "the expropriation of one's person," which involves "offering it to Christ for the salvation of men."[24] In doing so, one comes to participate in the communion between the Son and the Father:

> The sign of the Son is his communion with the Father. The Son introduces us into the Trinitarian communion, into the circle of eternal love, whose persons are "pure relations," the pure act of giving oneself and of welcome. The Trinitarian plan . . . shows the form of life of the true evangelizer—rather, evangelizing is not merely a way of speaking, but a form of living: living in the listening and giving voice of the Father.[25]

This trinitarian, interpersonal dynamic is not only the model for evangelization, but is also the reality to which each human being is called. Moreover, Benedict expresses this communion in terms of friendship. He insists that the Christian life does not mean

22. John Paul II, *Evangelium Vitae*, Introduction, 2.
23. Ratzinger, *New Evangelization*, para. 2.
24. Ratzinger, *New Evangelization*, para. 17.
25. Ratzinger, *New Evangelization*, para. 18.

reducing the gospel to moralism—i.e., to a mere humanistic regimen for moral improvement—for such a reduction "loses sight of the essence of Christ's message: the gift of a new friendship, the gift of communion with Jesus and thereby with God."[26] The vocation of those whom Benedict terms "new evangelizers" is to draw people to this new friendship by exhibiting to them the beauty of the gospel.[27] This beauty is most fully seen and experienced in communion with others:

> On this Way one never walks alone but in company, an experience of communion and brotherhood that is offered to all those we meet, to share with them our experience of Christ and his Church. Thus testimony combined with proclamation can open the hearts of those who are seeking the truth so that they are able to arrive at the meaning of their own life.[28]

This experience of communion and brotherhood enables the gospel to overcome the resistance of modern people, enabling those who sincerely seek the truth to discover it and thus escape the despair of nihilism so characteristic of contemporary secularism. Friendship, the most precious and noble form of this communion, is naturally suited to communicate this message. As Christians, we are called to "lead human beings out of the wilderness in which they often find themselves to the place of life, friendship with Christ that gives us life in fullness."[29]

If, for Pope Benedict, the drawing power of the gospel is beauty, then for Pope Francis the drawing power is joy. In his apostolic exhortation *Evangelii Gaudium*, Francis understands the vivifying power of joy, stemming from the good news of Jesus Christ, as the cutting edge of effective evangelization. This supernatural

---

26. Ratzinger, *New Evangelization*, para. 30.

27. One of the themes of Benedict's theology is the persuasive power of beauty, not only the beauty of the church's artistic patrimony, but also and especially, the beauty of her saints. See Benedict XVI, "Wounded by the Arrow of Beauty," 32–41.

28. Benedict XVI, *Homily of His Holiness*, para. 7.

29. Benedict XVI, *Homily of His Holiness*, para. 11.

joy addresses what Francis identifies as the great danger pervading our contemporary world, "the desolation and anguish born of a complacent yet covetous heart, the feverish pursuit of frivolous pleasure, and a blunted conscience."[30] It is in the encounter with the gospel that we experience that joy that emerges from friendship with God and are enabled to overcome the complacency and covetousness that weighs us down. Francis writes:

> Thanks solely to this encounter—or renewed encounter—with God's love, which blossoms into an enriching friendship, we are liberated from our narrowness and self-absorption. We become fully human when we become more than human, when we let God bring us beyond ourselves in order to attain the fullest truth of our being.[31]

Friendship with God liberates us from the self-imposed confinement of pride. It does so by elevating us beyond the confines of our created nature, taking us beyond the limits of our human nature in order to participate in God's own triune life. This participation, according to Francis, is "the fullest truth of our being," at the center of which is the integration of life and faith. Sadly, our secular, post-Christian culture has lost this integration. Judging from the writings of John Paul II, Benedict XVI, and Francis, what is needed is a reintegration of faith and life. This is what contemporary culture desperately needs. Christians must identify those elements of culture that facilitate the reception of the gospel, as well as those elements that hinder its reception. When we speak of transforming the culture, we mean the attempt on the part of Christians to do two things. First, Christians must identify and perfect those cultural phenomena that are compatible with the gospel, orienting them toward the salvation of souls. Second, we must critique and refute those phenomena that are contrary to the gospel, for these hinder the salvation of souls. Indeed, they work toward spiritual destruction. Friendship is a vital cultural good that can and must be recovered in order for the culture to be transformed

30. Francis, *Evangelii Gaudium*, 1.2.

31. Francis, *Evangelii Gaudium*, 1.8.

and reoriented to the salvation of souls. Moreover, I maintain that Christian friendship represents the integration of faith and life at its deepest level, and it is both the means of redeeming the culture and the greatest expression of culture thus redeemed.

This book proposes to study the intellectual trajectory of friendship from its origins in classical antiquity to the Renaissance. It will pay particular attention to the various historical understandings of friendship in light of the relational capacities of the human person created in the image of God. The Western tradition has a long and rich intellectual pedigree in the area of friendship. The classical tradition, represented in the writings of Plato, Aristotle, and Cicero, articulated the experience of friendship as the highest of human ideals, linking it indelibly with genuine human happiness. The Christian tradition not only perfected the insights of the classical thinkers, but also elevated friendship to a supernatural level, in much the same way as the natural virtues of prudence, justice, fortitude, and temperance, which are ordered to happiness in this life, become supernatural virtues when elevated by grace and redirected to happiness in the life to come.[32]

In the New Testament, particularly the Gospel of John, we see a dynamic relationship between friendship (*philia*) and the love of Christ (*agape*), one in which friendship brings to fruition the sacrificial nature of *agape*. In John Cassian, we see the connection between friendship and the ascetical life as it was practiced in early monasticism. Gregory Nazianzen's friendship with Basil of Caesarea echoes many of the themes of classical antiquity, particularly the vital role of the intellectual life in friendship, while these same themes are taken up and given a supernatural orientation. Ambrose of Milan takes up the Ciceronian understanding of the just man and reconfigures it through the use of biblical exemplars, concluding with a discussion of friendship as exemplified in various biblical figures and most perfectly embodied in Christ. Augustine, from the experiences he relates in the *Confessions*, relates in

32. Fr. Benedict Groeschal and Kevin Perotta discuss the relation between the natural and the supernatural virtues in their book, *Journey Toward God*, 54.

a powerful way the deleterious effects of sin on friendship and the truly intellectual and spiritual character friendship assumes in the life of a converted soul.

In the Middle Ages, we see the continuing development of the friendship tradition. *The Rule of St. Benedict*, with its emphasis upon interpersonal communion among the monks, who are admonished to serve Christ in each other, facilitates the emergence of a distinctly monastic type of friendship. Gregory the Great emphasizes friendship with God and the corresponding responsibility of the person to become a "soul-keeper" for his or her friend. In Anselm of Canterbury, we see monastic friendship in its most basic sense; it is a vital means whereby the soul achieves union with God. Aelred of Rievaulx takes this idea and brings it to perfection. He reflects upon Cicero's definition of friendship in the light of sacred Scripture and explicitly orients it to Christ, specifically through an allegorical application of the Song of Songs. Finally, Thomas Aquinas recovers the Aristotelian understanding of friendship, and by means of this argues persuasively that friendship is synonymous with the theological virtue of charity.

In the Renaissance, we notice a more robust recovery and reassertion of the classical friendship tradition. Petrarch's letters give perhaps the earliest glimpse of this recovery, which reveals an intense, intimate relationship not only between Petrarch and his contemporary, Boccaccio, but also—at least in the mind of Petrarch—an equally intimate bond with Cicero. In Erasmus of Rotterdam, we see how friendship plays a pivotal role in his *philosophia Christi*, which is the heart of his vision for the reform of church and society. Finally, Erasmus gives us a portrait of Thomas More as the personification of Christian friendship, both in the unreserved affability he showed to his intimates and in the goodwill he maintained toward his executioners.

The chapters that follow exposit the key texts of these thinkers, reflecting upon them in light of the relational understanding of the human person as the image of God. The concluding chapter attempts to integrate these reflections in a rudimentary vision of a "culture of friendship," which, I believe, provides the intellectual basis for Christian engagement with the culture. My hope is that this study will encourage ongoing research, discussion, and reflection on the nature of Christian friendship and its vital role in culture and society.

1

Friendship in Classical Antiquity

WHAT EXACTLY IS FRIENDSHIP? To answer this question, we must understand what friendship is *in esse*, as a natural, created good. To do this, we turn to antiquity. The classical idea of friendship was shaped very much by a culture that placed a premium on public life, on civic engagement and using one's talents and abilities in the service of the community. Even Socrates, known as the "gadfly" because of his pestering, even impertinent questioning of his fellow citizens about their understandings of justice, truth, and the good life, viewed his work as a form of service to his beloved Athens. As a final homage to his *polis*, Socrates even accepted death at the decision of his fellow citizens.

In such an intensely social context, it was natural for philosophers to explore the nature of friendship. The Greek word for friendship is *philia*, the basic meaning of which is "love, affection, fondness." Among the Greeks, *philia* was ordered to two things: the happiness of the persons involved and the good of the community.[1] Friendship could include not only close friends, but also family, and even favorably disposed acquaintances.[2] The common characteristic in all these relationships was a particular notion of justice, i.e., that one should benefit one's friends and harm one's

---

1. Baltzly and Eliopolous, "Classical Ideals of Friendship," 13.
2. Baltzly and Eliopolous, "Classical Ideals of Friendship," 12.

enemies.[3] We see this in the orator Lysias (ca. 445–ca. 380 BC). He recounts a speech given by an Athenian soldier in his own defense against a slanderous accusation. The soldier, Polyaenus by name, eloquently defends himself against his accusers. Near the conclusion of the speech, he urges the jurists in the case to render a just decision. The manner in which he expresses his hope underscores the commonly accepted understanding of friendship and justice:

> I have been only moderately angry at my opponents' unjust behavior, because I believed that life was organized on a principle of hurting one's enemies and helping one's friends. I should be far more grieved, however, if I were deprived of justice at your hands, because I shall be seen to have suffered this fate not because of personal enmity but because of something wrong in the city.[4]

Curiously, there is a very subtle connection here between justice and friendship. Justice, the virtue whereby we render to each person what is their due, is superseded by the principle of reciprocity: one should do good for one's friends and harm to one's enemies. One cannot expect good things, e.g., justice, from one's enemies. Polyaenus says that he expects unjust treatment from his enemies, but not from his fellow citizens who lack any personal animosity against him. He expects his fellow citizens to be just toward him, i.e., do good to him, because there is no enmity between them and himself. Justice is to be given only to one's friends and to those to whom one bears no animosity. It is not to be given to, or expected from, one's enemies. This, according to Polyaenus, is the principle for the ordering of life. Life is ordered according to interpersonal alliances constructed for mutual support and protection. Friendship was thus popularly understood to be a relationship formed for this purpose, what later thinkers would refer to as friendship of "utility." In this context, friendship was goodwill for those favorably disposed to oneself, and a corresponding animosity toward the ill-disposed. This might be called the conventional view of friendship held among the Greeks.

3. Baltzly and Eliopolous, "Classical Ideals of Friendship," 15.
4. Lysias, "For the Soldier," 9.19.

Plato

Plato (ca. 427–ca. 347 BC) critically explores and, in the person of Socrates, refutes this view. In the *Republic*, he takes the conventional view and turns it on its head. At a certain point in the dialogue, during a discussion of the nature of justice, one Polemarchus reiterates justice according to the accepted definition, "to give to each what is owed him."[5] He then applies this definition to friendship in such a way as to support the conventional view: "By all means one should give [one's enemies] what is owed to them. And in my view what enemies owe to each other is appropriately and precisely—something bad."[6] Socrates responds by challenging Polemarchus's understanding of friendship. He asks him to ponder the relationship between friendship and moral goodness: "Speaking of friends, do you mean those a person believes to be good and useful to him or those who actually are good and useful, even if he doesn't think they are, and similar with enemies?"[7] Polemarchus replies that a friend is one whom one believes to be good and useful, and the same with enemies.[8] Socrates then draws attention to the fact that we are often mistaken in this. We often perceive someone to be good, yet in reality they are bad; likewise, we perceive someone to be bad, when in fact they are good. If this is true, Socrates argues, then good people are often our enemies and bad ones our friends, and if this is so, then "it's just to benefit bad people and harm good ones."[9] This absurdity leads the two of them to redefine what a friend is: "A good person will be a friend and bad one an enemy."[10] Notice that friendship is now rooted in moral goodness. A good person is a friend, simply by virtue of being good. But Socrates goes even further. Given the fact that a good person is a friend simply by virtue of being good, he asks

5. Plato, *Republic*, 331e2.
6. Plato, *Republic*, 332b.
7. Plato, *Republic*, 334b7–c2.
8. Plato, *Republic*, 334c3–4.
9. Plato, *Republic*, 334c9–d1.
10. Plato, *Republic*, 335a.

if a truly good man can ever harm anyone, even his enemy.[11] Polemarchus responds that it is right to harm those who are bad and, therefore, enemies.[12] Socrates then shifts the focus to virtue (*arete*). *Arete* refers to "excellence" or "perfection." The virtue or *arete* of a horse is to be an excellent horse; of a dog, to be an excellent dog. The virtue of a human being, according to Socrates, is to be just, to be morally good.[13] Socrates then gets Polemarchus to acknowledge that things become worse when they are harmed: a horse becomes a bad horse, a dog becomes a bad dog. From this, it follows that "people who are harmed must become more unjust."[14] He then reaches an absurd conclusion: "Those who are just can make people unjust through justice,"[15] that is, by giving them the bad things they supposedly deserve. On the contrary, the role of the just person is to make others just. Socrates arrives at the conclusion that a just person must never do harm to anyone, be he friend or enemy. Since a just man is a good man, and it is the function of the good man to make others good, and since doing harm to someone does not make that person good, it is clear "that it is never just to harm anyone."[16] Thus, Plato repudiates the view of justice as doing good to one's friends and harm to one's enemies. Justice, on the contrary, does good even to an enemy in the hope of making the unjust person just. For Plato, à la Socrates, both friendship and justice are rooted in moral goodness.

Elsewhere Plato tells us that the good that provides the foundation for friendship is temperance, or self-control. We see this in his *Phaedrus*. The dialogue centers on the contention by Phaedrus that the services offered by a non-lover are preferable to those of a lover. The Greek word used here is *philos*, which can be translated "lover" or "beloved," but is also translated "friend." A friend is one who dearly loves another. In what does such love consist?

11. Plato, *Republic*, 335b2.
12. Plato, *Republic*, 335b3.
13. Plato, *Republic*, 335c3.
14. Plato, *Republic*, 335c5.
15. Plato, *Republic*, 335c11.
16. Plato, *Republic*, 335e4.

The question is rendered murky by the Athenian institution of *paiderastia*, a relationship between an older man and teenage boy, through which the younger partner was to learn virtue.[17] Ideally, such a relationship did not involve sexual activity, although it did involve *eros*, which for the Greeks signified a type of love characterized by longing for a good that one lacks. Erotic love is the desire to possess a good that is perceived to reside in a beloved object, yet calls the lover beyond the beloved to the contemplation of the good in its purest form. For Socrates, this ultimate good was truth itself, pure and unstained by physical desire. However, such a relationship often devolved into sexual activity on account of the passions that would often be aroused. For this reason, argues Phaedrus, the services of a non-lover/non-friend are preferable to that of the lover/friend. The lover is admittedly "out of his mind" because of his desire for his beloved, is given to possessiveness and jealousy, and "keeps his eye on the balance sheet—where his interests have suffered from love, and where he has done well."[18] In other words, the services of the lover come with strings attached. The services of the non-lover, however, "are not forced but voluntary; and he does the best that he possibly can for you, just as he would for his own business."[19] Moreover, it is physical arousal that specifically undermines genuine friendship. Phaedrus says:

> Lovers [*philoi*] generally start to desire your body before they know your character or have any experience of your other traits with the result that even they can't tell whether they'll still want to be friends with you after their desire has passed. Non-lovers, on the other hand, are friends with you even before they achieve their goal, and you've no reason to expect that benefits received will ever detract from their friendship for you.[20]

We immediately notice that friendship continues to involve the rendering of services. Phaedrus insists that such services, in order

17. Reeve, "Plato on Friendship and Eros."
18. Plato, *Phaedrus*, 231b.
19. Plato, *Phaedrus*, 231b.
20. Plato, *Phaedrus*, 233a.

to be genuine, must be disinterested. Socrates, for his part, acknowledges the soundness of Phaedrus's argument, but then challenges him by offering a defense of *eros*. *Eros*, Socrates acknowledges, is indeed a type of madness, but he maintains that "the best things we have come from madness, when it is given as gift of the god."[21] He asserts, "madness [*mania*] from a god is finer than self-control of human origin."[22] Does it follow for Socrates that yielding to the physical passions is a good thing? Not at all. Such yielding to sexual activity among lovers is a debasement of their relationship. This is because their *eros* is ordered to an ultimate end: the contemplation of truth. The mind of the true philosopher, the "lover of wisdom," ascends to contemplate divine, eternal truths. Such an ascension involves a recollection of eternal truths that the soul encountered in its pure spiritual state before it became joined to a body. Such a soul is "planted in the seed of a man who will become a lover of wisdom or of beauty."[23] Such a man, possessing such a soul, is one "who practices philosophy without guile or who loves boys philosophically."[24] His love for the other is ordered to a mutual apprehension of truth. Such a man "stands outside human concerns and draws close to the divine; ordinary people think he is disturbed and rebuke him for this, unaware that he is possessed by a god."[25] This is the madness seen in someone "when he sees the beauty we have down here and is reminded of true beauty."[26] In the relationship between the lover and the beloved, this recollection of eternal truth and beauty evokes *eros*, "erotic" desire for these two transcendent goods. Yielding to sexual temptation in such a relationship represents a falling short of the true ideal of love.[27] If the two persons yield to the lower appetites, to "ambition in place

---

21. Plato, *Phaedrus*, 244a9–10.

22. Plato, *Phaedrus*, 244d4.

23. Plato, *Phaedrus*, 248d3–4.

24. Plato, *Phaedrus*, 249a2–3.

25. Plato, *Phaedrus*, 249d1–3.

26. Plato, *Phaedrus*, 249d5.

27. I am indebted to my colleague Dr. Elliot Bartky for clarifying and confirming this observation.

of philosophy," their lack of discipline will "bring them to commit that act which ordinary people would take to be happiest choice of all."[28] If, on the other hand, the two devote themselves to philosophy, then their shared life becomes "one of bliss and shared understanding." They are "modest and fully in control of themselves now that they have enslaved the part that brought trouble into the soul and set free the part that gave virtue."[29] This, according to Socrates, is the true good of friendship, enjoyed by true "lovers," that is, lovers of wisdom. This good is far superior to the services bestowed by a non-lover/non-friend, which pays only "cheap, human dividends."[30] Thus, for Plato, a shared perception of the good invites the two friends to a lifelong relationship characterized by philosophy and virtue.

Aristotle

This emphasis upon a shared perception of and striving toward the good achieved a fuller and more systematic development in Aristotle (384–322 BC). In his *Nichomachean Ethics*, Aristotle discusses friendship (*philia*) in the context of the virtues, which are the basis of personal and political morality. For Aristotle, virtue (*arete*) is a strength of character arising from habit.[31] Such character strengths include prudence, justice, fortitude, and temperance (i.e., the four cardinal virtues), as well as liberality, wittiness, et al. They are a middle way, or a mean, between extremes: a deficit and an excess.[32] For example, courage is the mean between cowardice (a deficit) and foolhardiness (an excess). Liberality is the mean between miserliness and extravagance. The virtues are the ways in which we cultivate the good in human nature and thus achieve *eudaimonia*, "happiness." *Eudaimonia* not only refers to a subjective sense of satisfaction, but also carries the idea of flourishing, "living

---

28. Plato, *Phaedrus*, 256b7–c5.

29. Plato, *Phaedrus*, 256a7–b4.

30. Plato, *Phaedrus*, 256e3–6.

31. Aristotle, *Nicomachean Ethics*, 1103a15.

32. Aristotle, *Nicomachean Ethics*, 1107a5.

well and doing well."[33] The virtues are the fundamental means to human flourishing. In addition, given the social nature of human beings, the virtues are also how we contribute to the good of the community in which we live. A virtuous person is one who has achieved rational mastery of his passions and appetites, and is thus able to contribute to the rational order and stability of the state. For this reason, a good magistrate is one who passes laws conducive to the virtue of the citizens. Aristotle writes: "For the legislator makes the citizens good by habituating them, and this is the wish of every legislator; if he fails to do it well he misses his goal. [The right] habituation is what makes the difference between a good political system and a bad one."[34] Thus, a good legislator enacts laws that form virtuous habits in his citizens. Virtue thus provides the foundation for a well-ordered body politic.

Where does friendship figure in this? What is the relationship between friendship, virtue, and the good of the community? After an extended discussion of the various virtues, Aristotle begins to discuss the nature of friendship, and maintains that friendship is necessary for the enjoyment and security of happiness. Friendship is also the relational means whereby virtue becomes operative and beneficial to the community. Friendship becomes publically operative through the virtue of beneficence. Beneficence is simply the practice of doing good for others. It is essential to human happiness. As Aristotle writes,

> No one would choose to live without friends even if he had all the other goods. For in fact rich people and holders of powerful positions, even more than other people, seem to need friends. For how would one benefit from such prosperity if one had no opportunity for beneficence, which is most often displayed, and most highly praised, in relation to friends?[35]

The value Aristotle gives to beneficence underscores the social, and particularly public, orientation of human happiness. A genuinely

33. Aristotle, *Nicomachean Ethics*, 1095a20.

34. Aristotle, *Nicomachean Ethics*, 1130b3–7.

35. Aristotle, *Nicomachean Ethics*, 1155a5–11.

happy person is one who is able to effect good things for his or her fellow citizens and be publicly praised for so doing. Friends, those upon whom one can bestow good things, make this possible. Thus, friendship is the means whereby one is able to share one's material prosperity and receive public praise thereby. Friendship is also the means whereby one protects and safeguards material prosperity, and is the only recourse when one is in poverty.[36] Friendship, then, is for mutual support and receiving public praise from one's fellow citizens. This seems to suggest the utilitarian view of friendship. How then does friendship relate to virtue? According to Aristotle, virtue must be sought for its own sake.[37] But if one practices beneficence for reciprocal support or public praise, how then is one exercising beneficence as a virtue?

The particular virtue that truly tests whether we view friendship in terms of the genuine good or in terms of utility is justice. On the one hand, Aristotle maintains that friendship provides a social good superior to justice. "Friendship," he writes, "would seem to hold cities together, and legislators would seem to be more concerned about it than about justice. For concord would seem to be similar to friendship and they aim at concord above all."[38] On the other hand, Aristotle views friendship as the highest form of justice: "The justice that is most just seems to belong to friendship."[39] This is because friends not only give to each other what is their due, but actually go beyond mere reciprocal justice and seek the good of the other to the fullest. Thus, for Aristotle, friendship transforms justice into a virtue that goes beyond the mere rendering of just desserts to seek the genuine happiness of the other. In this way, friendship promotes concord within the community in a manner that mere justice cannot. It promotes genuine interpersonal, social concord.

If friendship promotes interpersonal concord, then the question arises as to the character requirements of friendship. Aristotle

36. Aristotle, *Nicomachean Ethics*, 1155a10–13.
37. Aristotle, *Nicomachean Ethics*, 1105a31–35.
38. Aristotle, *Nicomachean Ethics*, 1155a25.
39. Aristotle, *Nicomachean Ethics*, 1155a25.

asks, "Does friendship arise among all sorts of people, or can people not be friends if they are vicious?"[40] Friendship necessarily involves mutual, reciprocated goodwill.[41] What sorts of persons can genuinely share in this give-and-take of good will? To answer this question, Aristotle discusses three types of friendship, corresponding to three types of love: love of utility, love of pleasure, and love of moral goodness. Friendship of utility is a relationship in which each person seeks some end beyond the relationship itself, e.g., social advancement, wealth, power. This type of friendship, of course, does not last, for "when the cause of their being friends is removed, the friendship is dissolved too."[42] Friendship of pleasure likewise is an unstable type of friendship. In such a relationship, the friends pursue recreations that are mutually satisfying. This type of friendship, according to Aristotle, is prevalent among the young, "who are guided by their feelings" and pursue whatever is ready at hand.[43] Like friendship of utility, friendship of pleasure is quickly dissolved: "Hence they are quick to become friends, and quick to stop; for their friendship shifts with [what they find] pleasant, and the change in such pleasure is quick."[44] Both in friendship of utility and of pleasure, friendship is coincidental to the goal of the relationship. For this reason, the friendship lasts only as long as what is sought after lasts. Finally, there is friendship based upon the love of moral goodness. This may be called friendship of virtue. This is the truest type of friendship, "the friendship of good people similar in virtue,"[45] and has as its goal the mutual cultivation of good moral character. Each person wishes good to the other, not for the sake of pleasure or utility, but simply for the sake of the other.[46] This type of friendship is truly lasting, because virtue itself is lasting. Aristotle continues:

40. Aristotle, *Nicomachean Ethics*, 1155b11.
41. Aristotle, *Nicomachean Ethics*, 1155b30.
42. Aristotle, *Nicomachean Ethics*, 1156a20–25.
43. Aristotle, *Nicomachean Ethics*, 1156a30.
44. Aristotle, *Nicomachean Ethics*, 1156a30–35.
45. Aristotle, *Nicomachean Ethics*, 1156b5.
46. Aristotle, *Nicomachean Ethics*, 1156b10.

> Now those who wish goods to their friend for the friend's
> own sake are friends most of all; for they have this at-
> titude because of the friend himself, not coincidentally.
> Hence these people's friendship lasts as long as they are
> good; and virtue is enduring.[47]

Friendship of virtue, among those who have cultivated habitual dispositions toward moral excellence, is friendship in its essence. It arises spontaneously from those who have acquired virtue. Because of this, in loving the other, one actually loves what is good for oneself, "for when a good person becomes a friend he becomes a good for his friend."[48] Thus there emerges a natural reciprocity between friends, accompanied by a genuine equality: "Each of them loves what is good for himself, and repays in equal measure the wish and the pleasantness of his friend; for friendship is said to be equality."[49] At the same time, this reciprocal love is rooted in self-love, which is seen in the internal concord of the soul with its own self: "The excellent person is of one mind with himself, and desires the same things in his whole soul."[50]

Aristotle divided the human soul into three levels: the nutritive soul, the sensitive soul, and the rational soul.[51] The nutritive soul is that which is common to plants, animals, and human beings, and is capable of nourishment, growth, and reproduction.[52] The sensitive soul is common to animals and humans, and is capable of sense perception.[53] The rational soul, exclusive to humans, is capable of thought and understanding.[54] In the morally good person, all three levels of the soul are ordered toward the same good: "He wishes himself to live and to be preserved," he "finds it pleasant to spend time with himself," and "shares his own

---

47. Aristotle, *Nicomachean Ethics*, 1156b10.

48. Aristotle, *Nicomachean Ethics*, 1158a35.

49. Aristotle, *Nicomachean Ethics*, 1158a35.

50. Aristotle, *Nicomachean Ethics*, 1158a35.

51. Aristotle, *De Anima*, 413a23.

52. Aristotle, *De Anima*, 413a23.

53. Aristotle, *De Anima*, 413a23.

54. Aristotle, *De Anima*, 413a23.

distresses and pleasures."[55] "The decent person," writes Aristotle, "has each of these features in relation to himself, and is related to his friend as he is to himself, since the friend is another himself."[56] This is the inward state of the virtuous person.

Two things are worth noting here. First, in this passage, there emerges what will be one of the principle characteristics of friendship, both in the classical and Christian traditions: the friend as an "other self." Second, we have here in Aristotle a paradoxical connection between interpersonal and *intra*personal relationships. The internal concord of the soul with its own self renders the person capable of concord with others outside the self, and becomes externalized in friendship. The vicious person, on the other hand, is incapable of the self-love that is necessary for true friendship. Vicious people, writes Aristotle, "are at odds with themselves, and like incontinent people, have an appetite for one thing and a wish for another."[57] A vicious person is alienated from himself, the various levels of the soul being at odds with each other. For this reason, a vicious person cannot stand to be alone with himself. Aristotle continues:

> Vicious people seek others to pass their days with, and shun themselves. For when they are by themselves they remember many disagreeable actions, and expect to do others in the future; but they manage to forget these in other people's company. These people have nothing lovable about them, and so have no friendly feelings for themselves. Hence such a person does not share his own enjoyments and distresses. For his soul is in conflict, and because he is vicious one part is distressed at being restrained, and another is pleased [by the intended action]; and so each part pulls in a different direction, as though they were tearing him apart.[58]

---

55. Aristotle, *Nichomachean Ethics*, 1166a15–25.

56. Aristotle, *Nichomachean Ethics*, 1166a30.

57. Aristotle, *Nichomachean Ethics*, 1166b5.

58. Aristotle, *Nichomachean Ethics*, 1166b15–20.

Thus, for Aristotle, true friendship can only exist among the virtuous, for only a virtuous person truly loves himself and is thus able to extend this love to another person, one who is likewise virtuous. Yet even this involves a certain amount of pleasure. Based upon the principle that "nature appears to avoid above all what is painful and to aim at what is pleasant,"[59] even friendship based upon virtue necessarily involves pleasure, i.e., pleasure in one another's company: "People cannot spend their time with each other if they are not pleasant and do not enjoy the same things, as they seem to in the friendship of companions."[60] Aristotle continues:

> It is the friendship of good people that is friendship most of all, as we have often said. For what is lovable and choiceworthy seems to be what is unconditionally good or pleasant, and what is lovable and choiceworthy for each person seems to be what is good and pleasant for him; and both of these make one good person lovable and choiceworthy for another good person.[61]

In other words, virtuous people both recognize the inherent lovability and choiceworthiness of each other and—by virtue of the fact that they themselves are good—find the companionship of each other pleasant and good for themselves. Thus it is that pleasure, like justice, is subordinate to friendship when such friendship is grounded in virtue.

Finally, for Aristotle, genuine friendship rooted in virtue is total, even to the point of self-sacrifice. The virtuous person, by rightly loving himself, desires truly good things and to bestow them upon others: "Hence the good person must be a self-lover, since he will both help himself and benefit others by doing fine actions."[62] This will to do good for others extends to the point of even being willing to die for the friend. A virtuous person "labours for his friends and for his native country, and will die for them if he

---

59. Aristotle, *Nichomachean Ethics*, 1157b15.

60. Aristotle, *Nichomachean Ethics*, 1157b20.

61. Aristotle, *Nichomachean Ethics*, 1157b25.

62. Aristotle, *Nichomachean Ethics*, 1169a10.

must."[63] Yet even this reciprocates to the benefit of the one making the ultimate sacrifice:

> This is presumably true of one who dies for others; he does indeed choose something great and fine for himself. He is ready to sacrifice money as long as his friends profit; for the friends gain money, while he gains what is fine, and so he awards himself the greater good. He treats honours and offices the same way; for he will sacrifice them all for his friends, since this is fine and praiseworthy for him. It is not surprising, then, that he seems to be excellent, when he chooses what is fine at the cost of everything.[64]

Here we have an illustration of the idea of the friend as another self. The sign of genuine friendship—i.e., friendship between the virtuous—is that when one does what is truly good for the friend, one benefits from it as well, simply by virtue of the act itself. The most noble of such actions is sacrifice. To sacrifice wealth for the material well-being of a friend, when done simply for the purpose of helping the friend, redounds to the honor of the one performing the action. To sacrifice a public honor so that one's friend might enjoy the glory affords one the honor of having done such a thing for one's friend. Finally, to give one's life for the good of the friend has the recompense of the highest honor for the one making the sacrifice. For Aristotle, such virtuous friendships, characterized by total commitment to the welfare of the other, form the basis of genuine social concord.

Cicero

Now we turn to Marcus Tullius Cicero (106–43 BC). Cicero's approach to friendship is less abstract than Aristotle's, reflecting the pragmatic Roman temperament in contrast to the speculative cast of mind we encounter in the Greeks. He sets forth his

---

63. Aristotle, *Nichomachean Ethics*, 1169a20.
64. Aristotle, *Nichomachean Ethics*, 1169a25.

understanding of friendship in his *De Amicitia*. The work is written in the form of a dialogue among three men: Fannius, Scaevola, and Laelius. Laelius is a mature man reflecting upon his friendship with his now-deceased friend Scipio Africanus, who was an eminent Roman statesman, while Fannius and Scaevola are two young men seeking to discern the true nature of friendship from Laelius's experience. Cicero gives us a succinct definition of friendship: "Friendship [*amicitia*] is nothing else than an accord [*consensio*] in all things, human and divine, conjoined with mutual goodwill [*benevolentia*] and affection [*caritate*]."[65] This *consensio* (literally "to feel with") in all things human and divine is the cement that binds friends together. *Benevolentia* and *caritas* give this *consensio* a certain moral quality, more properly known as *virtus*, "virtue." Continuing in the tradition of Plato and Aristotle, Cicero believes that friendship is possible only among the virtuous, for "without virtue friendship cannot exist at all."[66]

It is virtue, moral goodness, that evokes the *caritas* or affection so essential to friendship. Contending against those who maintain that friendship arises from a desire for some sort of advantage or personal gain, Cicero maintains that friendship spontaneously ensues from virtue. Echoing Aristotle, he maintains that a virtuous person sees in his or her friend "a sort of lamp of uprightness and virtue."[67] "For there is nothing," Cicero continues, "more lovable than virtue, nothing that allures us to affection, since on account of their virtue and uprightness we feel a sort of affection even for those whom we have never seen."[68] Moreover, virtue induces one to seek out like-minded people for companionship. Cicero tells us that Laelius experienced this in regard to Scipio. Speaking through Laelius, Cicero writes:

> I, assuredly, had no need of him either, but I loved him
> because of a certain admiration for his virtue, and he,
> in turn, loved me because, it may be, of the fairly good

65. Cicero, *De Amicitia*, 5.19.
66. Cicero, *De Amicitia*, 6.20.
67. Cicero, *De Amicitia*, 8.27.
68. Cicero, *De Amicitia*, 8.27–28.

opinion which he had of my character; and a close association added to our mutual affection. Although many
and great advantages did ensue from our friendship, still
the beginnings of our love did not spring from the hope
of gain.[69]

Since friendship is rooted in virtue, it can never be a justification
for committing an unjust act. "It is no justification whatever of
your sin," writes Cicero, "to have sinned on behalf of a friend; for,
since his belief in your virtue induced the friendship, it is hard
for that friendship to remain if you have forsaken virtue."[70] Thus
there is an inseparable relationship between friendship and moral
goodness. As in Plato and Aristotle, so in Cicero, moral virtue is
the quality that evokes friendship. Moral goodness causes two virtuous souls to be united in an inseparable bond. If this goodness is
forsaken, the bond naturally collapses.

Moreover, the truth that friendship ensues from virtue points
us to an even more fundamental source for friendship: nature itself.
For Cicero and like-minded thinkers, *natura* does not refer to the
natural, biological world per se (although it includes this), but to
the transcendent and universal order of reality itself. Nature is thus
immutable and abiding. This quality of immutability is essential
to the moral law of our human nature, discovered by reason, and
to which the Western moral tradition later gave the name *natural
law*. Thus, the moral virtues—prudence, justice, temperance, and
fortitude—instill within the person dispositions reflecting natural
law, and thus are abiding character qualities. To support his argument that friendship is rooted in nature itself, Cicero observes certain tendencies in physical nature analogous to human friendship.
Citing Empedocles, Cicero writes, "In nature [*in rerum natura*]
and the entire universe, whatever things are at rest and whatever
are in motion are united by friendship [*amicitiam*] and scattered
by discord [*discordiam*]."[71] Inanimate elements are "naturally" (according to their nature) united together in a kind of friendship. It

69. Cicero, *De Amicitia*, 9.30.

70. Cicero, *De Amicitia*, 11.37.

71. Cicero, *De Amicitia*, 7.24.

is the nature of reality itself to be in concord. Cicero also relates a recent incident in which the naturalness of friendship manifested itself. It involved the performance of a play by one Marcus Pacuvius. In this play, two friends, one of whom was named Orestes, stood before a king. The king, not knowing the identities of the two men before him, and intending to kill Orestes, asked which of them was Orestes. The two friends, neither wishing to see the other killed, both claimed to be Orestes, upon which the audience "rose to their feet and cheered this incident in fiction."[72] "In this case," Cicero observes, "nature easily asserted her own power, inasmuch as men approved in another as well done that which they could not do themselves."[73] In other words, the spectacle of two friends being willing to die for each other evoked from the crowd a natural approbation. Genuine friendship thus emerges spontaneously from human nature. Cicero continues:

> In friendship there is nothing false, nothing pretended; whatever there is is genuine and comes of its own accord. Wherefore it seems to me that friendship springs rather from nature than from need, and from an inclination of the soul joined with a feeling of love rather than from calculation of how much profit the friendship is likely to afford.[74]

This feeling of love between friends is so strong, and so rooted in nature, that it produces perfect interpersonal communion between the two of them, a communion so strong that the friend becomes another self. "What is sweeter," asks Cicero, "than to have someone with whom you may dare to discuss anything as if you were communing with yourself?"[75] Indeed, this is perhaps the sweetest benefit of friendship, having someone to whom one can bare one's soul in complete and perfect confidence. Moreover, this interpersonal and *intra*personal communion is rooted in nature and evidenced in the animal kingdom. Animals, argues Cicero,

72. Cicero, *De Amicitia*, 7.24.
73. Cicero, *De Amicitia*, 7.24.
74. Cicero, *De Amicitia*, 7.27.
75. Cicero, *De Amicitia*, 6.22.

not only love themselves, but also seek out others of their own kind for the purpose of survival.[76] If this is the case for irrational creatures, "then how much more, by the law of his nature, is this the case with man who both loves himself and uses reason to seek out another whose soul he may mingle with his own as almost to make one out of the two!"[77] The natural inclination to join with another person, discovered by reason, leads the rational creature to seek out friendship.

Also by virtue of the fact that it emerges from immutable nature, friendship itself partakes of this immutability and has the character of being eternal: "Since nature is unchangeable, therefore real friendships are eternal."[78] This eternal quality gives rise in Cicero to another aspect of friendship: it provides a sense of immortality. The bond between friends is so strong that not even death can sever it. There is a real sense in which a deceased friend remains in the life of the one still living through the happiness his memory gives:

> Wherefore friends, though absent, are at hand; though in need, yet abound; though weak, are strong; and—harder saying still—though dead, are yet alive; so great is the esteem on the part of their friends, the tender recollection [*memoria*] and deep longing that still attends them.[79]

The strength of true friendship, that it exists for its own sake and is therefore unending, continues beyond the grave, offering consolation and joy to the surviving friend. *Memoria*, i.e., "recollection" or "remembrance," preserves the interpersonal bond that existed while the friend was still alive. The perpetuity of friendship thus enables the friends to participate in a certain immortality. Moreover, it is the virtue, the moral goodness of the friend, which gives to friendship this eternal quality: "For me, indeed, though he was

76. Cicero, *De Amicitia*, 21.81.

77. Cicero, *De Amicitia*, 21.81.

78. Cicero, *De Amicitia*, 9.32.

79. Cicero, *De Amicitia*, 7.23.

suddenly snatched away, Scipio still lives and will always live; for it was his virtue that caused my love and that is not dead."[80]

The *memoria* or remembrance of a friend further serves the good of the community, particularly posterity. *Memoria* was a value dear to classical culture in which a premium was placed upon the accomplishment of great deeds and their becoming part of the public memory, to be recounted regularly by succeeding generations and thereby becoming part of a shared cultural repertoire. In this connection, Cicero contrasts the Greek Socrates, remembered for his wisdom, with the Roman statesman Cato: "Take care not to give the precedence over Cato even to that man, whom, as you say, Apollo adjudged the wisest of men; for the former is praised for his deeds, the latter for his words."[81] Cicero applies this to friendship, speaking through the person of Laelius:

> I am not so much delighted by my reputation for wisdom . . . especially since it is undeserved, as I am by the hope that the memory [*memoria*] of our friendship will always endure; and this thought is the more pleasing to me because in the whole range of history only three or four pairs of friends are mentioned; and I venture to hope that among such instances the friendship of Scipio and Laelius will be known to posterity.[82]

True friendship not only benefits the two friends themselves, but also redounds to the moral instruction and edification of the community and of posterity. For Cicero, friendship is not a purely private matter, but an institution that serves the common good.

Conclusion

One of the things that draws modern readers to the writings of Plato, Aristotle, and Cicero is their keen insight into the human condition. Nowhere do we see this insight better than in their

---

80. Cicero, *De Amicitia*, 27.102.
81. Cicero, *De Amicitia*, 2.10.
82. Cicero, *De Amicitia*, 4.14.

discussions of friendship. They were acutely aware of the popular tendency to reduce friendship to mere utility, to an exchange of goods and services for personal advancement in the world. They recognized the poverty of such a view, that such friendships could not last and were therefore unable to provide the true, lasting support we seek in friendship. The main contribution of Plato to our understanding of friendship is that friendship is ordered to moral goodness, and is therefore only possible among the good. The two good friends then assist one another in the apprehension of truth and in the contemplation of the good. With Aristotle, we see a further development of this relationship between friendship and moral goodness. He too maintains that friendship is only possible among the virtuous. Moreover, since virtuous friends sincerely seek the happiness of the other, friendship founded upon virtue promotes genuine interpersonal communion and civic concord. The heart of this concord is the idea of the friend as an "other self." One wishes the same good for the friend as one wishes for oneself. This leads to the virtuous person being willing to die, if necessary, for the good of the friend. In Cicero, we see three characteristics of friendship. First, he emphasizes that friendship is rooted in nature, i.e., in our unchanging moral nature. Second, he affirms, along with Plato and Aristotle, that true friendship is possible only among the virtuous. Third, he adds his discovery that true friendship, through *memoria*, gives us a sense of immortality. Even this, moreover, is rooted in virtue, for it is the virtue of the deceased friend that never dies. Furthermore, this *memoria* of a virtuous friend becomes part of the public memory, thus fostering the moral instruction and development of succeeding generations. It is clear that the philosophers of antiquity discovered in friendship a multidimensional good that served not only the individuals themselves, but the community in which they and their successors lived.

2

Friendship in Christian Antiquity

WITH THE EMERGENCE OF Christianity and the founding of the church in the first century AD, we witness the appearance of a new ethos, a new moral sensibility, within Greco-Roman society. At the root of this ethos is *agape*. *Agape* was one of several words the Greeks used to convey the multifaceted human experience of love. *Eros* stood for love as longing; it involved a desire for a beloved object. *Storge* signified love as loyalty or devotion, e.g., the love one would have for one's country, one's family, etc. *Philia*, of course, signified friendship-love. *Agape* was originally a more general word meaning "some kind of love."[1] The New Testament writers took up this very general word and gave it a new, more specific, and much more noble meaning. In the New Testament, *agape* means love as sacrifice for the good of the other; love without regard to want, desire, or personal benefit. It signifies the self-giving, sacrificial love of Christ for the church. It is the type of love that ought to prevail among Christians, and is the love Christians ought to have even for their enemies, but also transforms the more conventional types as well. *Eros*, love characterized by desire and even passion, is disciplined and made more stable and lasting by *agape*.[2] *Storge*, that loyalty to country and family whereby a stable sociopolitical order is established, is made subservient to the sacrificial demands of

1. Kreeft, *Catholic Christianity*, 86.
2. Benedict XVI, *Deus Caritas Est*, 10–11.

agape and thereby kept from degenerating into political idolatry. How does *agape* affect *philia*? How does the love of Christ transform friendship? Before we can answer this question, we must explore how Christians of antiquity understood friendship.

The Gospel of John

In the New Testament, we principally encounter *philia* in the Gospel of John, where the Evangelist often uses *philia* and *agape* synonymously.[3] We see this in the story of the illness, death, and resurrection of Lazarus in John 11. When Jesus is on his way to Bethany, he encounters a messenger sent by Mary and Martha: "So the sisters sent to him, saying, 'Lord, he whom you love [*phileis*] is ill.'"[4] Two verses later, the text reads, "Now Jesus loved [*egapa*] Martha and her sister and Lazarus."[5] Later still, when Jesus is standing before Lazarus's tomb, we read, "Jesus wept. So the Jews said, 'See how he loved [*ephilei*] him.'"[6] Thus *agape*, *philia*, and their derivatives seem to convey a common idea of intense, devotional love. Undoubtedly, the most significant use of the two terms in the Gospel of John occurs in the Farewell Discourse (John 15). Here the interplay between *agape* and *philia*, and the interpenetration of their meanings, is made much more explicit:

> This is my commandment, that you love [*agapate*] one another as I have loved [*egapesa*] you. Greater love [*agapen*] has no man than this, that a man lay down his life for his friends [*philon*]. You are my friends [*philoi*] if you do what I command you. No longer do I call you servants, for the servant does not know what his master is doing; but I have called you friends [*philous*], for all that I have heard from my Father I have made known

3. Haraguchi, "*Philia as Agape*," 250.

4. John 11:3. Unless otherwise stated, all Scripture references in this book are from the RSV, Catholic Edition.

5. John 11:5.

6. John 11:35–36.

to you . . . This I command you, to love [*agapate*] one another.[7]

On the most basic level, the Farewell Discourse uses *agape* and *philia* interchangeably. At the same time, a close examination of the text reveals how they interrelate in such a way as to manifest the self-sacrificial nature of *agape*.[8] The greatest love (*agape*) is a love in which one lays down one's life for the beloved. This is the love Jesus has for the disciples, and he now commands them to love one another in the same self-sacrificial manner. This sacrificial love is directed toward one's friends (*philoi*). Jesus considers the disciples his friends (*philoi*) if they, in turn, obey his commandment and lay down their lives for one another, i.e., if they have *agape*-love for each other. To be a friend of Jesus is to love as he loves. This idea of laying down one's life as a manifestation of love receives its *denouement* in John 21, where Jesus challenges Peter to feed his "sheep":

> When they had finished breakfast, Jesus said to Simon Peter, "Simon, son of John, do you love [*agapas*] me more than these?" He said to him, "Yes, Lord; you know that I love [*philo*] you." He said to him, "Feed my lambs." A second time he said to him, "Simon, son of John, do you love [*agapas*] me?" He said to him, "Yes, Lord; you know that I love [*philo*] you." He said to him, "Tend my sheep." He said to him the third time, "Simon, son of John, do you love [*phileis*] me?" Peter was grieved because he said to him the third time, "Do you love me?" And he said to him, "Lord, you know everything; you know that I love [*philo*] you." Jesus said to him, "Feed my sheep."[9]

At first, this passage seems to convey the mere interchangeability of *agape* and *philia*. Clearly, the two terms continue to convey the shared idea of intense personal devotion. However, the conversation takes place after the passion, after Jesus has laid down his life for his friends (*philoi*). It is in light of this heightened meaning

7. John 15:12–15, 17.

8. For an excellent exposition and analysis of this, see Haraguchi's "*Philia* as *Agape*," 256–59.

9. John 21:15–17.

of *agape-philia* that the evangelist intends us to understand the exchange between Jesus and Peter. Jesus is conveying to Peter the fundamental requirement of genuinely loving him: solicitude for Jesus's followers. If Peter genuinely loves Jesus, he will take care of his disciples, he will "feed [his] sheep." Moreover, the following passage further indicates the ultimate cost of this love:

> "Truly, truly, I say to you, when you were young, you fastened your own belt and walked where you would; but when you are old, you will stretch out your hands, and another will fasten your belt for you and carry you where you do now wish to go." (This he said to show by what death he was to glorify God.) And after this he said to him, "Follow me."[10]

The ultimate cost of loving Jesus is martyrdom. If Peter truly loves Jesus, then he will feed his sheep by dying for them in a manner like unto the death of Jesus himself. He will demonstrate his friendship with Jesus by loving the disciples as Jesus has.

What we have in the Gospel of John is more than a mere interchangeability between *agape* and *philia*. John establishes their shared meaning of intense personal devotion in regard to Jesus's love for Mary, Martha, and Lazarus. In the Farewell Discourse, the sacrificial nature of *agape*, which would become its constitutive meaning in the New Testament and in the emerging Christian tradition, becomes apparent. *Philia* now signifies the relationship between Jesus and those for whom he will enact *agape* by laying down his life. He will lay down his life for his "friends" (*philoi*). Thus, a friend is one for whom one lays down one's life. Finally, in the discourse in John 21, we have the *denouement* of the narrative in which the evangelist develops the relationship between *agape* and *philia*. In this relationship, *philia* manifests the truly sacrificial nature of *agape*.

---

10. John 21:18–19.

John Cassian

During the first three centuries of the church's life, the union of *philia* and *agape* was most powerfully expressed in martyrdom. Indeed, Peter's own martyrdom, alluded to in John 21, can be considered the paradigm of this type of love. Martyrdom came to be seen as the height of Christian perfection. At the same time, even before the Roman persecutions ceased, during late antiquity an alternative way of perfection emerged: monasticism. In the monastic movement, the notion of "laying down one's life" took on a very different meaning, and was ordered toward one's direct encounter with God through asceticism. Monasticism emerged in the deserts of Egypt and the Middle East in the late third century AD. At first an individual undertaking, monasticism involved the withdrawal of the individual Christian from the distractions of regular social life for a life of prayerful and meditative isolation. This earlier form, known as eremitic monasticism, found literary expression in the lives and writings of the early desert fathers, the most widely known of whom was St. Antony of Egypt (ca. 251–356). Antony and others like him soon acquired the status of heroic disciples of Christ by virtue of their extreme asceticism rooted in prayer and scriptural meditation. It might seem paradoxical, even contradictory, to look for evidences of friendship in eremitic monasticism. Indeed, Antony does not seem to have cultivated any friendships.[11] While he had many admirers, and many more came to him for spiritual direction or were inspired by his example to undertake the monastic life themselves, he and others like him maintained a profound aloofness from human concourse. Indeed, the radical *metanoia* or conversion central to monastic life required an equally radical cutting off of all prior social attachments, including family, friends, and village.[12] Brian Patrick McGuire expresses it well: "When the desert fathers mention friendship, they usually mean friendships with the world, the world that had been left behind. Friendships could grow in the desert, but they were not sought

11. McGuire, *Friendship and Community*, 9.

12. McGuire, *Friendship and Community*, 3.

for their own sake but were forged in shared spiritual lives."[13] Friendships seemed to have ensued in spite of, not because of, the renunciation required by eremitic monasticism: "The more the desert fathers concentrated on cutting themselves off from each other, the more they came to know and understand each other."[14] Thus there emerged a type of relationship that superseded the traditional bonds of family and social life. Out of this ensued a distinctly monastic understanding of friendship, one centered upon the shared goal of life with God. This goal required the practice of *apetheia*, the removal of all passions for the sake of rational, spiritual peace.[15] While the monks of the desert forged relationships with one another, these ideally excluded the emotional affection characteristic of traditional friendship. The peace of mind sought by the desert monks excluded the cultivation of close personal friendships, even with other monks in the communities that inevitably emerged in their common undertaking.[16] Abbot Macarius urged his brother monks to "flee from men, stay in your cell, weep for your sins, do not take pleasure in the conversation of men."[17]

During this same period, there developed alongside eremitic practice a communal variant known as coenobitic monasticism. Inaugurated by Pachomius (ca. 290–346), coenobitic monasticism institutionalized monastic life around a written rule and under the guidance of an abbot. This deliberate communal life naturally facilitated the formation of personal friendships. If one was living in a community of monks, however, one was still urged to maintain a certain emotional distance from one's brothers, "to keep the frame of mind of the stranger . . . so as not to become too familiar with them."[18] The desire for friendship, however, woven as it is into human nature, continued within monastic communities despite this injunction. The task facing the abbots was to ensure that friend-

13. McGuire, *Friendship and Community*, 5.

14. McGuire, *Friendship and Community*, 11–12.

15. McGuire, *Friendship and Community*, 15.

16. McGuire, *Friendship and Community*, 16.

17. McGuire, *Friendship and Community*, 16.

18. Abbot Agathon, quoted in McGuire, *Friendship and Community*, 17.

ship had the proper foundation in virtue and was oriented toward life with God. We see this in the advice given by one Abbot Joseph, related to us by John Cassian (ca. 360–432/435) in his *Conferences*. Cassian undertook the monastic life while a youth in Bethlehem.[19] He later made two journeys to Egypt and became thoroughly knowledgeable of the eremitic and coenobitic monks in the region. In the years 414 or 415 he journeyed to Gaul, and in Marseilles founded two monasteries, one for men and one for women.[20] His *Conferences* are a Latin compilation of the spiritual advice given by various eastern abbots he encountered in his youth. One conference in particular, relating the wisdom of one Abbot Joseph, treats the subject of friendship. From the text, we infer that Joseph was the abbot of a community of monks. Cassian tells us that Joseph "was carefully trained in the eloquence of Greece," from which we can infer that he was familiar with the Greek philosophical discourse on friendship.[21] Cassian and a companion pay a visit to Joseph, who inquires whether they were blood relations.[22] Upon hearing that they "were united in a tie of spiritual and not carnal brotherhood," he begins his discourse on friendship.[23] It seems as though the renunciation of worldly relations was a prerequisite for learning about spiritual friendship.

This is supported by what immediately follows: Cassian summarizes various types of worldly friendships: that based upon "a previous recommendation"; that based upon "some bargain or agreement to give and take something"; that based upon "a similarity and union of business or science or art or study"; and finally, one based upon kinship, "where the union is from the instincts of nature and the laws of consanguinity, whereby those of the same tribe, wives and parents, and brothers and children are naturally preferred to others."[24] These types of friendship have two things in

19. Chiovaro, "Cassian, John," 205.

20. Chiovaro, "Cassian, John," 205.

21. Cassian, *Conferences*, 16.1.

22. Cassian, *Conferences*, 16.1.

23. Cassian, *Conferences*, 16.1.

24. Cassian, *Conferences*, 16.2.

common: they are found among both the good and bad, and they do not last forever.[25] Cassian is not suggesting, of course, that such friendships are insincere. He is merely pointing out that they do not last and are therefore of no help in the spiritual life. Indeed, such friendships, along with the security and solace they provide, must be renounced by one who would undertake the monastic regimen. Cassian then gives an elucidation of true friendship:

> There is one kind of love which is indissoluble [*insolu-bile caritatis*], where the union is owing not to the favour of a recommendation, or some great kindness or gifts, or the reason of some bargain, or the necessities of nature, but simply to similarity of virtue [*similitudo virtutem*] . . . This is true and unbroken love [*vera et indirupta dilectio*] which grows by means of the double perfection and goodness of friends [*amicorum perfectione ac virtute*], and which, when once its bonds have been entered, no difference of liking and disturbing opposition of wishes can sever.[26]

We notice that Cassian interchangeably uses two words for love: *caritas* and *dilectio*. *Caritas* is the Latin noun for *agape* which, as we have seen, signifies self-sacrificial love, love carried to the point of death. *Dilectio*, which basically means "delight," is the word most often used by Latin Christian writers to signify active *caritas*.[27] This *dilectio* lacks the instability we would associate with ordinary, fleeting delight in something that gives pleasure. It is stable, lasting, "true and unbroken" (*vera et indirupta*), rooted in *amicorum perfectione ac virtute*, literally "the perfection and virtue of friends." From this unbreakable *dilectio* emerges an equally unbreakable concord between wills. Cassian continues: "Love can only continue undisturbed in those in whom there is but one purpose and mind to will and refuse the same things."[28] In worldly

---

25. Cassian, *Conferences*, 16.2.

26. Cassian, *Conferences*, 16.3.

27. This is because *caritas* lacks a verbal form, whereas *dilectio* has the verbal form *diligo*. See Robson, "With the Spirit and Power of Elijah," 186.

28. Cassian, *Conferences*, 16.3.

friendship there is unity in likes/dislikes, unity in interests/occupations, and unity in blood relations, all of which are subject to change. Genuine friendship is grounded in the will, which is not actually subject to change (in the sense of some external factor inducing the change), but changes only by virtue of itself. Thus, if the will is steady, the friendship is unchanging.

Much of the remainder of the conference concerns the conditions under which the two wills of the friends can be kept firm. The first condition, of course, is good character, shared by both friends. This is achieved through asceticism, through the mortification of desire. Cassian writes:

> If you wish to keep this [unity of will] unbroken, you must be careful that having first got rid of your faults, you mortify your own desires, and with united zeal and purpose diligently fulfill that in which the prophet specially delights: "Behold how good and joyful a thing it is for brethren to dwell together in unity" [Ps 133:1].[29]

The passage from Psalm 133 does not signify unity of place, but of wills: "For with God the union of character, not of place, joins brethren together in a common dwelling, nor can unruffled peace ever be maintained where difference of will appears."[30] How then is this unity of wills achieved? Cassian lists six "foundations" of friendship. The first foundation consists in contempt for worldly possessions.[31] The rationale for this is quite simple: "How can he ever differ from his friend, for if he claims nothing for himself, he entirely cuts off the first cause of quarrel?"[32] The second foundation is for each man to "prune his own wishes" so as not to consider himself wise and prefer his own opinion to that of his brother, for "how can he arouse any incitement to contention, who has determined to trust not so much to his own judgment

---

29. Cassian, *Conferences*, 16.3.
30. Cassian, *Conferences*, 16.3.
31. Cassian, *Conferences*, 16.6.
32. Cassian, *Conferences*, 16.6.

as to his brother's decision?"[33] Third, the monk must recognize that every good thing "must come after the blessing of love and peace"; indeed, such a one will never admit anything that grieves his brother, since he believes "that nothing is more precious than the blessing of peace."[34] The fourth foundation is to recognize that there is never a good reason for anger: "On what grounds will he endure either to admit the rancour of vexation in himself or for it to remain in another, if his firm decision is that there cannot be any good ground for anger?"[35] The fifth suggests the commonplace of the friend as another self: the monk must "try to cure any wrath which a brother may have conceived against him however unreasonably, in the same way as he would cure his own, knowing that vexation of another is equally bad for him, as if he himself were stirred against another."[36] The sixth foundation provides a fitting conclusion to the section: the monk must "realize daily that he is to pass from this world," which "not only permits no vexation to linger in the heart, but also represses all the motions of lusts and sins of all kinds."[37] In this series of maxims, Cassian provides a fitting summary of the monastic ideal: beginning with contempt of the things of the world, the monk must learn to overcome the passions, chief of which is self-will, guided by the constant awareness of death and judgment. At the same time, this ideal is the foundation of friendship within the monastic community. Unity of wills, which is the essence of friendship, is achieved through the radical renunciation of one's own will. This renunciation is the basis of interpersonal communion and concord, and thus is the heart of true friendship.

Having laid a solid basis for friendship patterned after monastic self-renunciation, Cassian now discusses two different types of love: *agape* and *diathesis*. In this section, he provides an implicit defense and justification for particular friendships within a

33. Cassian, *Conferences*, 16.6.

34. Cassian, *Conferences*, 16.6.

35. Cassian, *Conferences*, 16.6.

36. Cassian, *Conferences*, 16.6.

37. Cassian, *Conferences*, 16.6.

monastic community. *Agape* is that love "shown to all men in general," including one's enemies, as well as that love shown especially "to them that are of the household of faith."[38] *Diathesis*, "affection" (*affectus*), is that which we have for those who "are united to us by kindred dispositions or by a tie of goodness."[39] While the former is commanded, the latter emerges spontaneously, either from nature or from affinity of temperament. Even affection, however, admits different grades and levels of intensity. We love our parents in one way, our spouse in another, our brothers and sisters in yet another, and our children in still another way, "nor is the love [*dilectio*] of parents toward their children always equal."[40] As an example of this, Cassian cites the patriarch Jacob's singular love of Joseph among his twelve sons. This was not a moral failing on Jacob's part, Cassian insists, "not that that good man his father failed in greatly loving [*diligeret*] the rest of his children, but that in his affection [*affectui*] he clung to this one."[41] Jacob loved all of his sons. Yet he had a more intense delight in Joseph "because he was a type of the Lord."[42] Cassian then sees this same idea in the New Testament: "This also, we read, was very clearly shown in the case of John the Evangelist, where these words are used of him: 'that disciple whom Jesus loved [*diligebat*].'"[43] As in the case of Jacob, Cassian tells us that this singular love for John did not indicate a lack of affection for the other disciples, but merely that Jesus's love for John was "a fuller and more abundant love towards the one, which his prerogative of virginity and the purity of his flesh bestowed upon him."[44] Citing the Song of Songs, "Set in order love [*caritatem*] in me" (2:4), Cassian considers such preferential love to be fully in accord with the Christian perfection monasticism seeks:

38. Cassian, *Conferences*, 16.14. The biblical quote is from Galatians 6:10.
39. Cassian, *Conferences*, 16.14.
40. Cassian, *Conferences*, 16.14.
41. Cassian, *Conferences*, 16.14.
42. Cassian, *Conferences*, 16.14.
43. Cassian, *Conferences*, 16.14.
44. Cassian, *Conferences*, 16.14.

> For this is true love set in order [*caritas ordinata*], which,
> while it hates no one, yet loves [*diligit*] some still more by
> reason of their deserving it, and which, while it loves [*di-
> ligat*] all in general, singles out for itself some from those,
> whom it may embrace with a special affection [*peculiari
> affectione*], and again among those, who are the special
> and chief objects of its love, singles out some who are
> preferred to others in affection [*affectui*].[45]

If even among the twelve apostles there was a preferential love (*affectus*), along the lines of *amicitia*, between Jesus and John, then,
for Cassian, such preferential friendships are permissible within a
monastic community characterized by charity, a general love for
all. At the same time, however, such preferential love is to be given,
not on the basis of one's personal likes and dislikes, but upon spiritual merit, as we see in the instances of the patriarch Joseph and
the apostle John.

Gregory Nazianzen

While monasticism continued for centuries to be seen as the privi-
leged way of Christian perfection, with its own distinct understanding of friendship, a more classical understanding continued
in the church as well. While *agape* was the characteristic form of
Christian love, *philia* still retained a place in the tradition, and, in
the hands of the church fathers, preserved something of its earlier meaning. We see this in Gregory Nazianzen's *Funeral Oration*
for Basil of Caesarea. Gregory Nazianzen, Basil of Caesarea, and
Basil's brother Gregory of Nyssa were together what later tradition named "the Cappadocian Fathers." The three of them, in
their writings and in their tireless efforts, advanced the cause of
orthodoxy in the eastern church during the doctrinal and political turmoil of the post-Nicene era. Gregory Nazianzen and Basil
cultivated a close friendship that provides us with an excellent example of the classical ideal in a Christian context. In the *Oration*,
Gregory recounts Basil's life, his parentage, their shared education

45. Cassian, *Conferences*, 16.14.

in Athens, and their later struggles to defend the faith against a heretical emperor. At the heart of his eulogy is a narrative of their friendship. In this narrative, we encounter many allusions to the classical understanding. Gregory understands their friendship to have consisted of "full accord of heart and nature,"[46] to entail certain obligations: "I have not failed through any negligence on my part to render what was due. Far be it from me to be so careless of the claims of virtue or friendship, or to think that the duty of praising him befitted anyone more than myself."[47] Most importantly, Gregory understands virtue to be constitutive of friendship: "When he was among us, he used to correct me on many points according to the rights of friendship and a still higher law. I am not ashamed to say this, for he was a norm of virtue for all."[48] Later, Gregory adds, "While he lived, he aided me in virtue."[49] Gregory and Basil's friendship is most fully illuminated, however, in light of their shared understanding of the purpose of education and intellectual life. Early in the discourse, as a sort of prelude to the story of their friendship, Gregory sets forth his pedagogical philosophy. It is a philosophy that sharply rejects an unthinking rejection of secular learning, "that external culture which many Christians by an error of judgment, scorn as treacherous and dangerous and as turning us away from God."[50] Gregory continues:

> On the contrary, we select from them what is useful both for life and enjoyment and we avoid what is dangerous, not opposing creation to the Creator, as the foolish do, but acknowledging the Maker of the world from His works, and as the holy Apostle says, bringing every mind into captivity to Christ.[51]

---

46. Gregory of Nazianzus, *Funeral Orations*, 39.

47. Gregory of Nazianzus, *Funeral Orations*, 28.

48. Gregory of Nazianzus, *Funeral Orations*, 28.

49. Gregory of Nazianzus, *Funeral Orations*, 46.

50. Gregory of Nazianzus, *Funeral Orations*, 35.

51. Gregory of Nazianzus, *Funeral Orations*, 35.

Here Gregory succinctly expresses the Christian appropriation of the Greco-Roman intellectual tradition initiated by the fathers of the church. It was to this ideal that he and Basil would commit themselves, and which provided the impetus for the growth of their friendship. This came to light during their time at Athens. Athens, even in late antiquity, was still known as a center of intense, even fierce, intellectual discourse, and like many such cities, hosted a rather unruly student life. Part of this life was a certain rite of passage. According to Gregory, it involved a rather boisterous berating of the newcomer, including a sometimes frightening procession to the public baths, where the newcomer would be further rattled by loud howling and yawping, finally ending with the newcomer's congenial reception as an equal.[52] Gregory, having arrived at Athens earlier, persuaded his classmates to spare Basil the ordeal on account of his "gravity of character and his maturity of judgment."[53] Gregory continues: "This was the prelude to our friendship. This was the spark that enkindled our union. It was thus that we were struck with a mutual love."[54] Soon after, another incident further cemented their friendship. It likewise involved their fellow students. Gregory tells us that there was a group of "Armeneans" who approached Basil "with the appearance of friendship, though prompted by envy, not benevolence."[55] Having heard of Basil's renown in argument and oratory, these set upon Basil with a barrage of philosophical questions and conundrums, "hoping to vanquish him at the first onset."[56] It was soon obvious that the Armeneans, even collectively, were no match for Basil. Gregory came to the aid of the Armeneans, initially believing their questions to have been posed in good faith. When their real intention became clear, however, Gregory joined forces with Basil:

> When I realized what was behind the discussion, for
> it could not be kept back, but eventually revealed itself

52. Gregory of Nazianzus, *Funeral Orations*, 40–41.

53. Gregory of Nazianzus, *Funeral Orations*, 40–41.

54. Gregory of Nazianzus, *Funeral Orations*, 41.

55. Gregory of Nazianzus, *Funeral Orations*, 41.

56. Gregory of Nazianzus, *Funeral Orations*, 41.

clearly, I changed my position immediately and, putting my ship about and ranging myself on his side, I made his victory decisive . . . And full of ardor, to describe him fully in the words of Homer, he drove in confusion those proud youths by his reasoning, and did not cease smiting them with arguments until he had completely routed them and gained a crowning victory. This was the second step in our friendship, no longer a spark but a flame that burned bright and high.[57]

Both Gregory and Basil were committed to Christian philosophy, the "bringing every mind into captivity to Christ." In the debating victory with the Armenean students, we see this shared commitment begin to emerge, not so much in terms of content, but in their ability to set at naught the presumption of lesser intellects.

Nevertheless, Gregory tells us that the experience caused Basil to become quickly disillusioned with Athens. He considered Athens an "empty happiness."[58] Gregory, for his part, sought to alleviate Basil's disappointment, telling him that just as the character of an individual cannot be known through a single encounter, so the character of a place or group cannot be known from only a few experiences.[59] "In this way," writes Gregory, "I restored his good spirits, and by this mutual experience I bound him to myself all the more."[60] Gregory's reasoned alleviation of Basil's disillusionment with Athens, combined with previously coming to Basil's aid in the trap set by the Armenean students, established them in the strong bond of friendship. As a result, Gregory and Basil became veritable soulmates. Philosophy being their shared endeavor, they were "all in all to each other."[61] They shared "the same roof, the same table, the same sentiments," their eyes "fixed on one goal."[62] Contrasting their relationship with carnal love, which is centered on things

57. Gregory of Nazianzus, *Funeral Orations*, 42.
58. Gregory of Nazianzus, *Funeral Orations*, 43.
59. Gregory of Nazianzus, *Funeral Orations*, 43.
60. Gregory of Nazianzus, *Funeral Orations*, 43.
61. Gregory of Nazianzus, *Funeral Orations*, 43.
62. Gregory of Nazianzus, *Funeral Orations*, 43.

ephemeral and passing, the love shared by Gregory and Basil was centered on that which is enduring.[63] In this, Gregory echoes the Socratic ideal of genuine, chaste friendship:

> But those loves which are pleasing to God, and chaste, since they have a stable object, are on that account more lasting, and, the more beauty is revealed to them, the more does it bind to itself and to one another those whose love is centered on the same object. This is the law of the higher love.[64]

Carnal love, for Socrates and for Gregory, is a dangerous counterfeit to the "higher love" of friendship. True friendship is lasting, and only a lasting good can sustain it.

Gregory's and Basil's friendship eventually came to be tested, however. Basil's intellectual abilities and personal holiness soon came to be recognized universally, and he was called upon to become bishop of Caesarea. One of the characteristics of the classical idea of friendship, as the Greeks and Romans understood it, was the mutual obligation to advance each other's social, professional, economic, and even political interests. While genuine friendship was not based upon such favors (in which case it degenerated into a false, utilitarian friendship), such advantages nevertheless were expected to ensue even from friendship between virtuous people. Moreover, the society of antiquity was permeated by this culture of mutual beneficence and service. As the church became increasingly intertwined with social and political life, it too began to be affected by this culture. Thus, there was a general expectation that Gregory, a known friend of Basil, would naturally advance with him. Gregory writes:

> How his philosophy squared with my own at the time! Everyone thought that I would rush forward after his accession with great joy—as anyone else, perhaps, might

---

63. Gregory of Nazianzus, *Funeral Orations*, 43.
64. Gregory of Nazianzus, *Funeral Orations*, 43.

have acted—and would share his power rather than rule beside him. Our friendship led men to surmise this.[65]

Gregory, however, resisted this temptation, and remained where he was.[66] Basil was initially hurt by Gregory's refusal but, being of one mind with his friend, came to respect and admire Gregory's decision.

In the conclusion of the oration, Gregory alludes to two other characteristics of classical friendship. First, in his lament over the loss of his friend, he suggests a variant of the idea of the friend as another self: the friend as one's "better half":

> Now he is in heaven, and there in our behalf, I am certain, he offers sacrifice and prays for the people. Though he has left us, he has not wholly left us. But I, Gregory, who am half dead and cut in two, now that our great union is sundered, drag out a painful life, a natural result of my separation from him.[67]

Of course, Gregory feels as though part of his own self has been taken away by the death of his friend. In addition, Gregory says that Basil "has not wholly left us," alluding to the idea, particularly strong in Cicero, that one's deceased friend continues to live on in one's memory. However, in this same passage, we encounter a distinctly Christian idea, i.e., that the friend, now a saint, intercedes for his still-living friends. Basil continues his priestly office in heaven, offering sacrifices for those he has left behind. It is in this capacity, not merely in the memory, that Basil has not entirely left his friend.

Ambrose of Milan

We see the classical ideal in a different light in Ambrose of Milan's *De Officiis* (*On Duties*). Written in three books, *De Officiis* is addressed to the clergy as an extended discussion of the moral

---

65. Gregory of Nazianzus, *Funeral Orations*, 61.

66. Gregory of Nazianzus, *Funeral Orations*, 61.

67. Gregory of Nazianzus, *Funeral Orations*, 97.

responsibilities of those undertaking the priesthood. Ambrose, having been trained in the Roman rhetorical tradition, models the work on an identically titled treatise by Cicero, and yet it departs significantly from the classical tradition, relying overwhelmingly on biblical examples of various virtues.[68] This is something characteristic of patristic literature: the taking up of classical ideals and then presenting them as having been more perfectly exemplified in sacred Scripture as opposed to the Greco-Roman literary tradition from which they derive. In this way, classical ideals are elevated, even transformed, by divine revelation. Ambrose's discussion of friendship occurs at the very end of Book Three, the topic of which is the relation between the honorable and beneficial.[69] Ambrose prefaces the topic with a discussion of the nature of a just man, using biblical examples. The most important characteristic of the just man is communion with self. The first exemplar of this is David:

> The prophet David taught us that we should walk around in our heart as though we were in a spacious house, and commune with it as we would with a good companion. This is what he did himself. He used to talk to himself and hold conversations with himself, as he tells us in his own words: "I have said: I will guard my ways."[70]

Ambrose follows with the examples of Solomon and Moses. Solomon advises making use of the counsel within one's own heart: "Use your own counsel. 'The counsel that lies in the heart of man is deep water. Let no stranger share it with you.'"[71] Moses likewise expresses this truth: "There on the mountain for forty days, he received the whole of the law. And in that time of solitude he was hardly without someone to talk to."[72] Ambrose presents Elisha as one who accomplished great things in solitude by virtue of his companionship with God: he divided the Jordan and passed through

---

68. McGuire, "Ambrose, St," 339.

69. Ambrose, *De Officiis*, 3.8.

70. Ambrose, *De Officiis*, 3.1.

71. Ambrose, *De Officiis*, 3.1. The quote is from Proverbs 20:5.

72. Ambrose, *De Officiis*, 3.2.

on foot; on Mount Carmel, he enabled a barren woman to con-
ceive; he brought the dead back to life; he made bitter food sweet;
he fed a multitude with ten loaves; he recovered an iron ax-head
from the depths of a river; he cleansed a leper; he "turns drought
into rain, turns famine into fruitfulness."[73] Ambrose concludes:

> So when is the just man ever alone? He is always with
> God. When is he ever on his own? He is never separated
> from Christ. "Who shall separate us," asks the apostles,
> "from the love of Christ? I am confident that neither
> death nor life nor angel can ever do so."[74]

Thus, the just person communes with his own self and, in so doing, communes with Christ. This is because Christ is present in the
depths of his soul.

It is from this understanding of the just person that Ambrose
embarks upon his consideration of the honorable and the beneficial. In this, he contrasts the wisdom of the world with divine wisdom, that is, "perfect wisdom," which in turn forms the basis for
discerning what is honorable. "The just man," he writes, "has no
interest in anything except what is lasting and honourable."[75] He
adds this: "for we are not following the wisdom of the flesh, which
can think of no higher benefit than financial gain: we are following
the wisdom which comes from God, which counts the things that
are considered great in this world as loss."[76] Those things which
one might customarily consider to be of great personal benefit—
e.g., money, prestige, honor, power—are pursued by one "who is
wise in the common sense of the word." Contrariwise, the wisdom
of God teaches one to put the benefit of others before one's own
benefit. One who possesses this divine wisdom is "perfectly wise"
and "concentrates all his attention on something else entirely—on

---

73. Ambrose, *De Officiis*, 3.6.
74. Ambrose, *De Officiis*, 3.7.
75. Ambrose, *De Officiis*, 3.7.
76. Ambrose, *De Officiis*, 3.7.

what is eternal, on what is seemly and honourable," that is, what will benefit all.[77]

Moreover, Ambrose maintains that this mandate of perfect wisdom—that is, seeking the honorable for the benefit of others— is rooted in our human nature. Here he exposits even further his understanding of the essentially communal nature of the human person. Again, contrary to what people customarily believe, the truly "natural" thing is to put others before oneself:

> Think, man, how you acquired your name, *homo*, "man". It comes, of course, from *humus*, "the earth". Now the earth takes nothing from anyone—far from it: she shows great generosity in giving everything to everyone alike, and she supplies all her different fruits to be enjoyed by all living things. So the quality of *humanitas*, "humanity", is the virtue that is specific and natural to man, for it is all about man helping those who share the same nature as himself.[78]

This obligation to help others "is undoubtedly the law of nature [*lex naturae*], which binds us to all humanity [*ad omnem stringit humanitatem*]."[79] Ambrose carries his argument further by alluding to the Pauline metaphor of the body in relation to the church. "We are born in such a way," he writes, "that members fit with other members, and each attaches itself to another, and all serve one another. If one fails in its duty, the rest are impeded."[80] Continuing with the metaphor, Ambrose draws an explicit connection between the interdependence of humanity and the one body of Christ:

> If when one member is treated that way the entire body is violated, then it stands to reason that when one whole man is treated that way it is the community that is destroyed. It is the nature of the human race that is

77. Ambrose, *De Officiis*, 3.12.

78. Ambrose, *De Officiis*, 3.16. Ambrose's derivation of *humanitas* from *humus* is not without precedent. See Pincombe, *Elizabethan Humanism*, 23n5.

79. Ambrose, *De Officiis*, 3.19.

80. Ambrose, *De Officiis*, 3.19.

violated—and so too is the whole congregation of the holy church [*violatur natura generis humani et sanctae ecclesiae congregatio*], for it rises into one body, joined and bound together in the unity of faith and love. And Christ the Lord, who died for all, will be grieved, for it will seem that the price of his blood has been paid in vain.[81]

Ambrose sees an implicit relationship between the oneness of humanity and the oneness of the church. The Latin expresses this relationship in the parallelism *violatur natura generis humani et sanctae ecclesiae congregatio*. The "congregation of the holy church" (*sanctae ecclesiae congretatio*) and "the nature of the human race" (*natura generis humani*) share the verb "violated" (*violatur*). To violate the communion of persons on the natural level violates interpersonal communion on the supernatural level as well. The violation, in fact, is so grave that Christ himself is grieved at the prospect of his sacrifice having been in vain.

The bulk of the remainder of Book Three consists of biblical exemplars of this principle that the honorable consists in seeking the genuine benefit of others, even at the cost of great peril or even one's life. Examples include David, who twice had opportunity to kill his persecutor King Saul, but refused to do the dishonorable thing and raise his hand against the Lord's anointed;[82] Judith, who single-handedly ended the Assyrian siege of Jerusalem by sheer force of personality, "By showing such a seemly disregard for her own safety, she brought the siege with all its dangers to an end, and by acting so honourably in a personal capacity she secured an outcome that was beneficial for the people as a whole";[83] John the Baptist, who refused to "turn a blind eye to a union which was dishonorable, even if it involved a king," and suffered a martyr's death;[84] and Esther, who risked death in order to rescue her people

81. Ambrose, *De Officiis*, 3.19.
82. Ambrose, *De Officiis*, 3.33–34.
83. Ambrose, *De Officiis*, 3.84–88.
84. Ambrose, *De Officiis*, 3.89.

from the genocide plotted by Haman.[85] This last example provides a point-of-departure for Ambrose's discussion of friendship. The Persian king executed Haman, "his second-in-command, the man he had counted chief among all his friends."[86] Haman had given the king "deceitful advice" and treated him dishonorably.[87] Ambrose then begins his discussion of friendship, which forms the conclusion of the treatise:

> Friendship [*amicitia*] is only commendable, you see, when it preserves what is honourable [*honestatem*]. Friendship must come before wealth, or honour [*honoribus*], or power, certainly, but it is not normal that it should come before what is honourable [*honestatem*]; rather, it should follow it.[88]

It is important to understand the difference between two Latin words for honor: *honestas* and *honor*. *Honor* refers to public esteem or praise; *honestas* denotes respectability, honesty, and integrity. The former, of course, ranks among what is sought by worldly wisdom; the latter is the goal of perfect wisdom and is the governing quality of genuine friendship. Ambrose then provides David's friend Jonathan as an example of this: "He had such a sense of loyalty, he did not shrink from incurring his father's displeasure or from endangering his own life for the sake of it."[89] The remainder of Ambrose's exposition follows this same pattern: the classical ideal reflected in a biblical exemplar revealing the ideal in a more perfect form. True friendship never demands dishonesty or perjury on behalf of the friend, but is subordinate to the common good:

> Scripture does say this: "Like a club, a sword, or an arrow of sharpened iron, so is the man who bears false witness against his friend." But notice what Scripture is declaring here. It is not the giving of evidence against a friend

---

85. Ambrose, *De Officiis*, 3.124.

86. Ambrose, *De Officiis*, 3.124.

87. Ambrose, *De Officiis*, 3.124.

88. Ambrose, *De Officiis*, 3.125.

89. Ambrose, *De Officiis*, 3.125.

as such that is being condemned: it is the giving of false evidence. For what if the cause of God or the interests of our country compel a person to give evidence? Should friendship count for more than religion? Should it count for more than love for your fellow-citizens?[90]

Friendship must also be enduring: "Friendship ought to be constant, and its feelings ought to last. We must not behave like children, changing our friends just on the basis of a vague whim."[91] Friendship also involves coming to the aid of the friend in hardship:

> Do not forsake a friend in need, do not desert him, do not fail him, for friendship is an aid to life. That is how we bear one another's burdens, as the apostle taught us to do—for his words are addressed to those who have been embraced by the same love of friendship.[92]

The biblical allusion here is Paul's letter to the Galatians: "Bear one another's burdens, and so fulfill the law of Christ."[93] Here we notice Ambrose subtly introducing an important distinction in his understanding of friendship. In Galatians, Paul is clearly addressing the whole Christian community, urging them to support one another as members of the body of Christ. He is imploring them to practice basic Christian charity, which is directed to all without distinction. It is this selfless service to others that fulfills the "law of Christ." Yet Ambrose sees in this same passage the essence of friendship, which by nature is not shared indiscriminately, but is reserved for those of like mind, temperament, and virtue. This suggests a transformation and even a universalization of friendship. All Christians, by virtue of their common life in Christ, are friends to one another.

The most important characteristic of friendship for Ambrose, however, is loyalty. This is where Christianity truly perfects the classical ideal. Ambrose writes: "Open your heart to your friend,

---

90. Ambrose, *De Officiis*, 3.127. The biblical quote is from Proverbs 25:18.
91. Ambrose, *De Officiis*, 3.128.
92. Ambrose, *De Officiis*, 3.129.
93. Gal 6:2.

so that he will be faithful to you, and so that you will know joy in your own life from him: For 'a faithful friend is the medicine of life,' the grace of immortality."[94] In addition, Ambrose reiterates the ideal of the intimate friend as another self: "You unite your innermost being to his, you join your spirit to his, you blend so thoroughly with him that your aim is no longer two, but one. You entrust yourself to him as to another self."[95] In this spirit Ambrose gives advice to his priests:

> So, my sons, take good care of the friendship you have entered into with your brothers . . . It really is a comfort in this life to have someone to whom you can open your heart, someone with whom you can share your innermost feelings, and someone in whom you can confide the secrets of your heart; to have at your side a man who will always be faithful to you, someone who will rejoice with you when things are going well, sympathize with you when circumstances are hard, and encourage you in times of persecution. Think of those Hebrew boys, and what good friends they were! Not even the flames of the fiery furnace could sever them from their love for one another . . . Well did holy David say: "Saul and Jonathan were so splendid, so precious: inseparable they were in life, and in death they were not separated."[96]

Loyalty enables one to bear one's soul to the friend without fear. It safeguards genuine interpersonal communion. While we see this powerfully exemplified in the friendship among Hananiah, Mishael, and Azariah and between Saul and Jonathan, its perfect realization, according to Ambrose, is found in the relationship between Christ and the apostles. Referring to John 15, Ambrose says that God "makes us his friends" and has given us "the pattern of friendship": we are "to do whatever our friend wishes, open up to

94. Ambrose, *De Officiis*, 3.129. The biblical quote is from Sirach 6:16.

95. Ambrose, *De Officiis*, 3.134.

96. Ambrose, *De Officiis*, 3.132. The reference to the "Hebrew boys" derives from Daniel 3, the story of three of Daniel's friends whom the Babylonian King Nebuchadnezzar threw into a fiery furnace for refusing to worship an image of the king.

our friend every last secret we have in our heart."[97] This particular aspect of friendship, that of interpersonal intimacy, of sharing the secrets of one's heart with one's friend, becomes particularly important. Ambrose continues:

> We must show him our heart, and he must open his heart to us. "I have called you friends," Jesus says, "because everything I have heard from my Father I have made known to you." A friend hides nothing, then, if he is true: he pours out his heart, just as the Lord Jesus poured out the mysteries of the Father.[98]

Ambrose takes what is perhaps the most precious aspect of the classical ideal of friendship and elevates it to a transcendent level. Through friendship with Christ, one is able to enjoy an intimate, inner conversation with God himself in which God shares his innermost secrets with the soul. Christ hides nothing from the soul to whom he is befriended. Here we see the heightened importance of solitude discussed at the beginning of Book Three: it is the setting that makes this inner conversation with Christ possible.

This hiding of nothing, this total self-disclosure, requires total trust, which of course entails the possibility of betrayal. In this connection, Ambrose presents the treachery of Judas as the ultimate exemplar of false friendship: "He who is one with [God] in spirit is also his friend, for there is a unity of spirits among friends, and there is no one more detestable than the individual who damages this friendship."[99] Ambrose views the gravity of Judas's betrayal precisely in these terms:

> So, when the Lord confronted the one who betrayed him, this was the thing he found worst of all about his treachery, this the crime he condemned most of all—the man had shown no gratitude at all for all that he had received, but had mixed his evil poisons while sitting at the very table of friendship. This was why the Lord spoke as he did: "But it was you, a man who was one with me

97. Ambrose, *De Officiis*, 3.136.
98. Ambrose, *De Officiis*, 3.136.
99. Ambrose, *De Officiis*, 3.137.

in spirit, my guide and my companion, you who always took sweet food with me." His point, in other words, was this: "This is what I find so unbearable: it was you, who lay in wait for me—you who were one with me in spirit!"[100]

Moreover, Judas's betrayal was, in reality, a betrayal of his own self: "[Jesus] said, 'But it was you, a man who was one with me in spirit.' In other words: 'I am not the one who is betrayed: you have betrayed yourself, for you have betrayed a man who was one with you in spirit.'"[101] Ironically, in the very act of betrayal, Judas reveals the heart of friendship: the communion of persons of such intensity that the friend becomes another self. Thus, to turn on one's friend is to turn on oneself.

Augustine

In Augustine we encounter an experience-based understanding of the classical ideal, one powerfully affected by his understanding of the deleterious effects of sin in human relationships. In the earlier chapters of his *Confessions*, he relates his experiences of friendship during the years of his wayward youth when he was driven by disordered desire (*concupiscentia*). Concupiscence affected Augustine on many levels, but his most intense desire was "to love and to be loved."[102] This uncontrolled desire permeated the friendships of his youth, leading him to sin, even to commit acts that he would otherwise not have committed.[103] In his view, such friendship cultivates disordered desires, which in turn confuse our moral reasoning.[104] Augustine's most intense discussion of friendship, however, occurs in Book Four. While a young man at his home town of Thagaste, Augustine formed a close bond with a youth of

100. Ambrose, *De Officiis*, 3.137.

101. Ambrose, *De Officiis*, 3.137.

102. Augustine, *Confessions*, 2.2.

103. The incident of the pear tree theft is a singular example of this, according to Tamer Nawar. See Nawar, "*Adiutrix Virtutum*," 202–4.

104. Nawar, "*Adiutrix Virtutum*," 202–4.

his own age. He describes the relationship as "a very sweet experience, welded by the fervour of our identical interests," and "sweet to me beyond all the sweetness of life that I had experienced."[105] At the same time, Augustine qualifies the experience by denying it the status of true friendship, not because it was founded upon utility or pleasure, but because it lacked a foundation in Christ: "It was less than a true friendship [*vera amicitia*] which is not possible unless you bond together those who cleave to one another by the love which 'is poured into our hearts [*caritate diffusa in cordibus nostris*] by the Holy Spirit who is given to us' (Rom. 5:5)."[106] Why did Augustine consider this to be inauthentic friendship? It possessed the characteristics identified by the philosophers. He and his friend enjoyed "identical interests"; they depended emotionally upon each other's company: "My soul could not endure to be without him"[107]; they were soulmates: "He was my 'other self.' Someone has well said of his friend, 'He was half my soul.' I had felt that my soul and his soul were 'one soul in two bodies.'"[108] Augustine discovers the inauthenticity of the friendship in his own reaction when his friend dies. After scarcely a year his friend took sick. His family had him baptized while unconscious. When he recovered, he and Augustine were estranged from each other. Augustine, now in the clutches of Manicheism, mocked the baptism. His friend, however, had embraced it: "But he had already learnt that he had received the sacrament. He was horrified at me as if I were an enemy."[109] Something profound had come between the two friends: grace. His friend was now indelibly linked to Christ and thus estranged from Augustine. A few days later, the fever returned and his friend died. Augustine was so overcome with grief that he became inconsolable. Every place, every association, every memory evoked grief:

105. Augustine, *Confessions*, 4.7.

106. Augustine, *Confessions*, 4.7.

107. Augustine, *Confessions*, 4.7.

108. Augustine, *Confessions*, 4.11.

109. Augustine, *Confessions*, 4.8.

> Everything on which I set my gaze was death. My home town became a torture to me; my father's house a strange world of unhappiness; all that I had shared with him was without him transformed into a cruel torment. My eyes looked for him everywhere, and he was not there. I hated everything because they did not have him, nor could they now tell me "look, he is on the way," as used to be the case when he was alive and absent from me.[110]

Here we see a very striking dissimilarity between Augustine and Cicero, specifically having to do with *memoria*. Whereas for Cicero the memory of the deceased is consoling to the point of almost making him present despite his absence, for Augustine this memory intensifies his sorrow. Augustine tells us that his grief was so intense that he began to experience a sense of self-alienation, something he was only able to express many years later during the intense introspection of the *Confessions*: "I had become to myself a vast problem, and I questioned my soul 'Why are you sad, and why are you very distressed?' But my soul did not know what reply to give."[111] Later in the narrative, he writes:

> I had become to myself a place of unhappiness [*infelix locus*] in which I could not bear to be; but I could not escape from myself. Where should my heart flee to in escaping from my heart? Where should I go to escape from myself? Where is there where I cannot pursue myself? And yet I fled from my home town, for my eyes sought for him less in a place where they were not accustomed to see him.[112]

The loss of his friend had made the young Augustine unable to be in his own presence. He had become to himself *infelix locus*, an "unhappy place." Yet, in his experience of self-alienation, Augustine also came to experience a deeper level of self-knowledge:

> I was in misery, and misery is the state of every soul overcome by friendship with mortal things [*amicitia rerum*

110. Augustine, *Confessions*, 4.9.
111. Augustine, *Confessions*, 4.9.
112. Augustine, *Confessions*, 4.12.

mortalium] and lacerated when they are lost. Then the soul becomes aware of the misery which is its actual condition even before it loses them.[113]

Human friendship had become a source of misery for Augustine because it inordinately tied him to the passible nature of created things. This *amicitia rerum mortalium*, the intimate attachment to things bound to pass away, leads not to joy but to sorrow. Here is where friendship reveals our true condition, wounded by sin and characterized by loving lesser goods as if they were the highest Good, the creature as if it were the Creator: "The reason why that grief had penetrated me so easily and deeply was that I had poured out my soul on to the sand by loving a person sure to die as if he would never die."[114] He then reflects upon his grief in the light of the God he would later discover to be the highest Good, for the sake of whom one ought to love all else:

> The lost life of those who die becomes the death of those still living. "Happy is the person who loves you" (Tobit 13:18) and his friend in you [*et amicum in te*], and his enemy because of you [*inimicum propter te*] (Matt. 5:44). Though left alone, he loses none dear to him; for all are dear in the one who cannot be lost.[115]

At this point in the story, however, Augustine had not yet fully learned the lesson. He resorted to the consolation of his remaining friends, again relying upon the creature instead of the Creator: "The greatest source of repair and restoration was the solace of other friends, with whom I loved what I loved as a substitute for [God]."[116] In this connection, Augustine echoes the classical view of friendship derived particularly from Cicero:

113. Augustine, *Confessions*, 4.11.

114. Augustine, *Confessions*, 4.13. Nawar puts it very well: "Augustine seems to think that *amicitia* deserves special attention insofar as it is especially adept at alleviating the symptoms of the human predicament and distracting one from the seriousness of one's condition" (Nawar, "*Adiutrix Virtutum*," 209).

115. Augustine, *Confessions*, 4.14.

116. Augustine, *Confessions*, 4.14.

There were other things which occupied my mind in the company of my friends: to make conversation, to share a joke, to perform mutual acts of kindness, to read together well-written books, to share in trifling and in serious matters, to disagree though without animosity—just as a person debates with himself—and in the rarity of disagreement to find the salt of normal harmony, to teach each other something or to learn from one another, to long with impatience for those absent, to welcome them with gladness on their arrival. These and other signs come from the heart of those who love and are loved and are expressed through the mouth, through the tongue, through the eyes, and a thousand gestures of delight, acting as fuel to set our minds on fire and out of many to forge unity. This is what we love in friends.[117]

This, of course, is a veritable litany of the pleasures of genuine friendship. For Augustine, these are genuine goods, and give us reason to praise God: "Let these transient things be the ground on which my soul praises you (Ps. 145:2), 'God creator of all.'"[118] Given the fact that human nature is wounded by sin, however, there is a natural tendency to love these goods as if they were the highest Good, and thus make of friendship an idol. These created goods, lacking permanence, "rend the soul" when they are taken away:

For these things pass along the path of things that move towards non-existence. They rend the soul with pestilential desires; for the soul loves to be in them and take its repose among the objects of its love. But in these things there is no point of rest: they lack permanence.[119]

The only corrective to this is for the loves of the soul to be rightly ordered. This is achieved when we love others, including our friend, for the sake of God, the highest Good and only abiding object of love. The theological virtue of charity—i.e., the love of God for God's own sake and the love of the friend for the sake of

117. Augustine, *Confessions*, 4.13–14.
118. Augustine, *Confessions*, 4.15.
119. Augustine, *Confessions*, 4.15.

God—is the only abiding foundation for friendship. This is because charity rightly orders human relationships. With Augustine, we thus encounter a subtle yet profound correction of the Ciceronian ideal. For Cicero, true friendship is characterized by a perpetuity that outlasts even death, continuing on in the quasi-immortality of memory. For Augustine, only a friendship rooted in charity is worthy of the name, for charity alone renders the friendship truly lasting.

Did Augustine ever experience genuine friendship? Despite his negative assessment of the friendship of his youth, he recognizes some intimations of this in his friendships prior to his conversion: "Among our group of friends we had had animated discussions of a project: talking with one another we expressed detestation for the storms and troubles of human life, and had almost decided on withdrawing from the crowds and living a life of contemplation."[120] Here we see a move toward a shared interest in eternal things, and thus toward a lasting foundation for friendship. While the specific project of forming a philosophical commune collapsed, Augustine tells us that he still enjoyed the fruits of genuine friendship with his philosophically minded associates: Nebredius, Verecundus, and Alypius. Nebredius in particular, he tells us, honored the obligations of friendship by agreeing to assist Verecundus in his teaching duties:

> So Nebredius was not attracted to this work by desire for profits; for had he so wished, he could have made more money on his own as a teacher of literature. He was a most gentle and kind friend, and recognizing the duty of generosity would not scorn our request.[121]

We notice here a particular aspect of this friendship: Nebredius rejects the love of temporal things, i.e., money, for the sake of a more lasting good, his friendship with one who shares his love of literature. While this falls short of charity, it is nevertheless a move away from passing goods toward that which is more lasting.

120. Augustine, *Confessions*, 6.14.
121. Augustine, *Confessions*, 8.6.

After Augustine's conversion, his intellectually based friendships were raised to a more sublime level. We see this first with Alypius. In Book Eight, Augustine relates the well-known story of his emotionally intense conversion. The setting is particularly significant. Up to this point, Augustine had been experiencing profound inner turmoil, torn between his attachment to his life of sensuality and the attraction of grace. Augustine was sitting with his friend Alypius, and his misery had become unbearable. He tells us that "a profound self-examination had dredged up a heap of all my misery and set it 'in the sight of my heart' (Ps. 18:15)."[122] This was immediately followed by "a massive downpour of tears."[123] He continues as follows:

> To pour it all out with the accompanying groans, I got up from beside Alypius (solitude seemed to me more appropriate for the business of weeping), and I moved away to ensure that even his presence put no inhibition on me. He sensed that this was my condition at that moment. I think I may have said something which made it clear that the sound of my voice was already choking with tears. So I stood up while in profound astonishment he remained where we were sitting.[124]

With his literary skill, Augustine presents the all-too-human experience of weeping. When we are overcome with tears, we feel embarrassment. We feel as though we must apologize for publically displaying our grief. Augustine likewise felt he must leave Alypius's presence in order to weep "properly." He wanted to ensure that even the presence of his friend would not inhibit Augustine's emotional need to vent through tears. One would think, of course, that their friendship would itself have provided a suitable venue for weeping. Nevertheless, Augustine felt that he must separate from his dear friend in order to give full issue to his sorrow.

Augustine tells us that he threw himself under a fig tree and let his tears flow freely: "Rivers streamed from my eyes, a sacrifice

122. Augustine, *Confessions*, 8.12.

123. Augustine, *Confessions*, 8.12.

124. Augustine, *Confessions*, 8.12.

acceptable to you (Ps. 50:19)."[125] His weeping was interrupted by the sound of a child singing "'Pick up and read, pick up and read.'"[126] Augustine took this to be a sign from God, returned to where Alypius was sitting, and opened a book of Paul's letter to the Romans and read the first passage he saw: "'Not in riots and drunken parties, not in eroticism and indecencies, not in strife and rivalry, but put on the Lord Jesus Christ and make no provision for the flesh in its lusts' (Rom. 13:13–14)."[127] Upon reading this, Augustine felt himself released from the grip of his sins. He then returned to Alypius:

> With a face now at peace I told everything to Alypius. What had been going on in his mind, which I did not know, he disclosed in this way. He asked to see the text I had been reading. I showed him, and he noticed a passage following that which I had read. I did not know how the text went on; but the continuation was "Receive the person who is weak in faith" (Rom. 14:1). Alypius applied this to himself, and he made that known to me. He was given confidence by this admonition. Without any agony of hesitation he joined me in making a good resolution and affirmation of intention, entirely congruent with his moral principles in which he had long been superior to me.[128]

We notice several things in this moving account. First, we sense how close is the friendship between Augustine and Alypius. While Augustine is going through the travails of spiritual suffering, his friend Alypius is there sitting quietly with him. He gives Augustine the consolation of his presence. Second, after his experience of liberation and his newfound peace, Augustine relates this intensely personal experience to Alypius. This, of course, indicates Cicero's idea of a friend as one to whom one can bare one's soul.[129] Finally,

125. Augustine, *Confessions*, 8.12.

126. Augustine, *Confessions*, 8.12.

127. Augustine, *Confessions*, 8.12.

128. Augustine, *Confessions*, 8.12.

129. Cicero, *De Amicitia*, 6.22.

desiring to continue their friendship on this higher, spiritual level, Alypius indicates his intention to follow Augustine into the Christian faith, joining his friend "in making a good resolution and affirmation of intention." Later, Augustine praises God for having subjected Alypius, "my heart's brother [*fratrem cordis*], to the name of your only-begotten Son, our Lord and Saviour Jesus Christ (2 Pet. 3:18)."[130] The interpersonal communion between Augustine and Alypius reaches its fullest expression in this shared resolution to embrace the faith.

In the case of Verecundus, we see a certain tension, even anxiety come upon his friendship with Augustine and Alypius as a result of their conversion. This was because "he was firmly tied by the chains of his obligations and saw himself losing our society."[131] The obligation consisted in the fact that he was married. Although his wife was a Christian, Augustine notes that Verecundus did not wish to become a Christian "except in the way which was not open to him," that is, as an ascetic.[132] He was fearful that Augustine's conversion would mean the end of their friendship: "We comforted Verecundus in his sadness by the fact that my conversion did not put an end to our friendship, and we exhorted him to faith appropriate to his rank, that is, to married life."[133] When Augustine was away in Rome, Verecundus took sick, received baptism, and died.[134] Augustine drew no small consolation from the fact that Verecundus had become a Christian before his death: "We would have felt tortured by unbearable pain if, in thinking of our friend's outstanding humanity to us, we could not have numbered him among your flock."[135]

Finally, we come to Nebridius. Nebridius, like Augustine, was a Manichean, but one who "was an ardent seeker after truth."[136]

130. Augustine, *Confessions*, 9.4.

131. Augustine, *Confessions*, 9.3.

132. Augustine, *Confessions*, 9.3.

133. Augustine, *Confessions*, 9.3.

134. Augustine, *Confessions*, 9.3.

135. Augustine, *Confessions*, 9.3.

136. Augustine, *Confessions*, 9.3.

Soon after Augustine's conversion and baptism, Nebridius "became a baptized Catholic believer."[137] Sometime later, Augustine tells us, Nebridius died: "Now he lives in Abraham's bosom (Luke 16:22). Whatever is symbolized by 'bosom', that is where my Nebridius [*Nebridius meus*] lives, a sweet friend to me [*dulcis amicus meus*], but, Lord, your former freedman and now adopted son [*tuus adoptivus filius*]."[138] Augustine refers to his friend as "my Nebridius," whom he calls a "sweet friend to me" but now "[God's] adopted son. The rhymed endings in the Latin suggest a parallel relationship between the Nebridius who belongs to Augustine and the Nebridius who now belongs to God: *Nebridius meus . . . amicus meus . . . tuus adoptivus filius*. Nebredius has gone from being Augustine's friend to God's adopted son. And yet he remains "my Nebridius" for Augustine all the same. Their friendship has been elevated to a more sublime level. Moreover, the interpersonal services that once characterized their relationship have likewise been transformed. Augustine tells us that Nebridius used to question him about divine things. Augustine was Nebridius's intellectual benefactor. Now that Nebridius is in heaven, however, the relationship has changed:

> There he lives; for what other place could hold so remarkable a soul? There he lives, in that place concerning which he used to put many questions to me . . . He no longer pricks up his ears when I speak, but puts his spiritual mouth to your fountain and avidly drinks as much as he can of wisdom, happy without end. I do not think him so intoxicated by that as to forget me, since you, Lord, whom he drinks, are mindful of us.[139]

Nebridius was a seeker of truth. What brought him and Augustine into such a close friendship was Nebridius's recognition of Augustine as one who could provide him with sound, illuminative direction in his search. Now that Nebridius is in God's presence, however, he no longer needs this from Augustine. He now drinks

137. Augustine, *Confessions*, 9.3.

138. Augustine, *Confessions*, 9.3.

139. Augustine, *Confessions*, 9.3.

freely from the font of wisdom. Moreover, we see here a transformation of Ciceronian *memoria*. In Cicero's thought, *memoria* provides a sense of immortality to the departed friend in that he continues to exist in the recollection of his surviving friends. In this way, the friend is never truly gone, and can continue to provide the consolation of his presence, albeit not in bodily form. For Augustine, the emphasis is not upon his memory of Nebridius, but upon Nebridius remembering Augustine. The consolation is Augustine's own certainty that Nebridius, by virtue of their shared relationship in Christ, remembers him. Because Christ is mindful of the surviving friends, the departed friend remembers them by virtue of Christ.

Conclusion

In the early centuries of the history of the church, we see a very real transformation of friendship. The Gospel of John gives friendship a new foundation in *agape*, sacrificial love for the good of one's brothers and sisters in Christ. The early monastic tradition took such self-sacrifice and recast it in terms of the achievement of personal holiness in the quest for direct communion with God. Yet even this profoundly individualist way allowed for genuine friendships to emerge, friendships characterized by shared virtue and a common spiritual pursuit. Many of the characteristics of friendship identified and exposited by Plato, Aristotle, and Cicero came to be more explicitly adopted by the Christian tradition. There is the idea that friendship consists in a community of shared interests. A friend continues to be understood as another self. There is the belief that genuine friendship is rooted in virtue, which in turn grounds the relationship in that which is abiding, as opposed to illusory friendships, which depend upon things that pass away. There is a genuine intellectual, even "cerebral" dimension to friendship, in that genuine friends are engaged in a shared attempt to comprehend the Good. Finally, there is an emphasis upon *memoria* as a solace for the survivor when his or her friend has died, the consolation that the departed friend lives on in the memories of his surviving friends and even in the collective memory of the community.

Christian thinkers, however, transformed and even went beyond the contributions of their Greco-Roman forebears. John Cassian takes the idea of shared interests and transposes it into a monastic milieu. The shared interest of the friends is their common quest for union with God, and it is a union that requires the renunciation of desire for the sake of interpersonal concord. Gregory's and Basil's relationship represents the cerebral dimension of friendship, grounded in Christian philosophy, the "bringing every mind into captivity to Christ." Ambrose not only transplants classical ideas into a more perfect scriptural setting, but also reinforces the conviction that friendship is only possible among the honorable, and that the most important characteristic of honor is loyalty. Ambrose elevates this loyalty to a transcendent level by rooting it in the soul's conversation with Christ. Christ communicates every intimate secret to the soul he has befriended, and, given the fact that the friend is another self, to betray Christ is to betray oneself. In Augustine's sad experiences of loss, we see human friendship assessed in light of God as the highest Good: "'Happy is the person who loves you' and his friend in you, and his enemy because of you." This becomes what might be called the "Augustinian principle" of friendship: friendships take on their true and lasting value in the context of our relationship with God. We will encounter this principle in subsequent chapters.

Finally, in Gregory and Augustine we see a radical transformation of *memoria*. While both experience profound grief at the loss of their friends, both are likewise convinced that the true solace offered by *memoria* resides, not in the survivor's memory of the departed friend, but in the friend's memory of the survivor, as the friend now enjoys perfect intimacy with Christ and is now able to communicate some measure of this intimacy to the surviving friend by virtue of their membership in the communion of saints.

3

Friendship in the Middle Ages

As any historical narrative of the period will testify, the time of
late antiquity was a time of upheaval. The Roman Empire in the
West—increasingly weakened by civil strife, economic stagnation,
and internal military conflict—disintegrated, culminating in its
formal dissolution in 476 AD. Despite the sociopolitical chaos
that characterized the disintegration of Roman order, however,
the intellectual legacy of the church fathers, which had taken up
and transformed Greco-Roman ideas, was preserved and developed in the Middle Ages. The ancient understanding of friendship
found new expression among medieval thinkers. In the current
chapter, we will explore how the idea of friendship developed in
the theological tradition of the medieval West, beginning with the
Benedictine monastic tradition and culminating in the thought of
Thomas Aquinas.

Benedict of Nursia

Benedict of Nursia (ca. 480–ca. 547) is credited as the founder of
western monasticism, due to the almost universal adoption of his
Rule. In the previous chapter, we encountered a discussion of monastic friendship from the eastern tradition in the *Conferences* of
John Cassian, according to whom the renunciation of desire and
one's own will is the means of achieving interpersonal concord,

which is the precondition of friendship. According to Cassian, one could argue, monasticism makes genuine friendship possible. At the same time, it has been argued that coenobitic monasticism has historically discouraged friendship, seeing such particular relationships as harmful to the solidarity of the community.[1]

The *Rule* of Benedict, concerned as it is with the proper spiritual formation of the individual monk and concord within the community, nowhere uses the term *amicitia*. Still, coenobitic monasticism is inherently relational, and thus one would expect a certain tendency toward friendship to be found within the Benedictine tradition. In the section discussing what the *Rule* calls "the instruments for good works," the monk is urged "to prefer nothing to the love of Christ" (*nihil amori Christi praeponere*).[2] *Amor Christi* refers to a spirit of sacrificial love for others.[3] The text then further exposits the nature of this in what follows. The monk is "not to give way to anger"; he is "not to nurse a grudge"; he is "not to entertain deceit in [his] heart"; he must "never give a false peace" or "forsake charity"; he must "utter truth from heart and mouth"; he must "do no wrong to anyone" and must "bear patiently wrongs done to [himself]"; he is "to love [his] enemies"; he is "not to curse those who curse [the brothers], but rather to bless them"; and he is "to bear persecution for justice's sake."[4] Here the *Rule* echoes the instruction found in Cassian, where friendship explicitly involves renunciation of anger and enduring any and all vexation one experiences at the actions of another. We notice that these are fundamentally relational admonitions, forming the monk in terms of his relationship with his brother monks. In addition, the *Rule* gives very specific instructions on how to treat guests and infirm brothers. In both cases, there is the admonition to recognize Christ in the other. In the section on the reception of guests, the *Rule* states this: "Let all guests who arrive be received

1. Southern, *Saint Anselm*, 140.
2. Southern, *Saint Anselm*, 140.
3. Kardong, *Benedict's Rule*, 85.
4. Benedict, *Rule for Monasteries*, 4.

like Christ, for He is going to say, 'I came as a guest, and you received Me' (Matt. 25:35)."[5] The text continues:

> In the salutation of all guests, whether arriving or departing, let all humility be shown. Let the head be bowed or the whole body prostrated on the ground in adoration of Christ, who indeed is received in their persons [*Christus in eis adoretur qui et suscipitur*]. After the guests have been received and taken to prayer, let the Superior or someone appointed by him sit with them. Let the divine law be read before the guest for his edification, and then let all kindness [*humanitas*] be shown him.[6]

The welcoming monks are to treat each visitor as Christ to such an extent that they pay him homage: Christ is "adored" (*adoretur*) and "received" (*suscipitur*) in them. The guests are invited to pray. They then receive instruction in sacred Scripture, after which they are treated to the kindness and hospitality of the community. Interestingly, the Latin term used here for "kindness" is *humanitas*, which, as we saw in Ambrose's *De Officiis*, primarily means "human nature," but also conveys the more abstract quality of the "human," that is, those qualities and ideals that pertain to humankind. Derived from this root meaning, *humanitas* also refers to humane conduct, i.e., gentleness, kindness, and generosity. Thus, the hospitality shown to the guest is a concrete expression of monastic solicitude for the fundamental human goodness and dignity of the person.

The language of the *Rule* becomes even more relational in regard to how the monks are to treat brothers who are ill. The sick, like the visitors, are to be treated in the same manner as Christ. In addition, the wording expresses a certain reciprocity between persons, suggesting something akin to friendship:

> Before all things and above all things, care must be taken of the sick, so that they will be served as if they were Christ in person; for He Himself said, "I was sick, and you visited Me" (Matt 25:36), and, "What you did for

5. Benedict, *Rule for Monasteries*, 13.

6. Benedict, *Rule for Monasteries*, 13.

one of these least ones, you did for Me" (Matt. 25:40). But let the sick on their part consider that they are being served for the honor of God, and let them not annoy their brothers who are serving them by their unnecessary demands.[7]

The first thing we notice in this passage is that care for the ill *must* be put "before all things and above all things." It is an absolute moral obligation to put the sick first. This moral imperative is a recognition of Christ in the sick brother. Yet there is an element of reciprocal concern here as well, for the sick brother is to be mindful of the fact that his brothers serve "for the honor of God" and therefore must respect their limitations and not make unreasonable demands. The healthy brothers are to serve their sick brother as if he were Christ, and the sick brother, mindful of this, is to act as Christ and keep his demands mild, remembering that Christ's yoke is easy and his burden light.[8] It is the presence of Christ in the sick person which effects a mutual humanization of the relationship between the one who serves and the one who is served, which is a very tangible restoration of the interpersonal communion characteristic of the image of God in the person. Thus, despite the distrust of intimate friendships that sometimes characterized the monastic movement, the *Rule* of Benedict reaffirmed the essentially relational and humanizing elements of the friendship tradition and thus facilitated the emergence of more explicit expressions of friendship later in the monastic tradition.

---

7. Benedict, *Rule for Monasteries*, 36.

8. Sr. Aquinata Böckmann identifies this reciprocal recognition of Christ in the practice of washing the feet of those entering and leaving the refectory: "Benedict has the brothers who have served for a week or who will serve the following week perform this rite. In this way they are to grow in the attitude of Christ, who washed the feet of the disciples (Jo 13). Christ is present in those who do the washing. But it seems to me that in the patristic texts commenting on the foot-washing, something additional is emphasized, that it is an honor for one to wash the feet. Christ serves in those who serve and he is served." See Böckmann, "Approaching Christ," 21–38.

Pope Gregory the Great

One of the first medieval thinkers to discuss friendship explicitly was Gregory the Great (ca. 540–604). Before he became pope in 590, Gregory had been a civil administrator of high rank, and then a monk following Benedict's *Rule*. In his *Dialogues* he composed the first biography of Benedict, and even in his capacity as bishop he maintained an affinity for the monastic tradition wherein his spiritual life had matured. At the same time, Gregory is known for his eminently practical and pastoral approach to theology, as evidenced in his treatise *Pastoral Care*. His *Gospel Homilies*, preached mainly during the early years of his pontificate (591–592), reveal a synthesis of monastic rigor and pastoral sensitivity.[9] One of his homilies treats specifically of friendship, both friendship between human beings and, more to Gregory's point, friendship with God. The topic is the friendship passage from the Farewell Discourse in John 15:12–16.[10] Gregory begins by stressing the fact that love is a commandment. Indeed "all of our Lord's utterances contain commandments."[11] Moreover, "whatever is commanded is founded on love alone."[12] Gregory's discussion of friendship occurs within this context:

> Our Lord's commandments are then both many and one: many through the variety of the works, one in their root which is love. He himself instructs us to love our friends in him, and our enemies for his sake. That person truly possesses love who loves his friend in God [*amicum diligit in Deo*] and his enemy for God's sake [*inimicum diligit propter Deum*].[13]

In this passage Gregory echoes the Augustinian principle of friendship: "'Happy is the person who loves you' (Tobit 13:18) and his friend in you [*et amicum in te*], and his enemy because of you

9. See the introduction of Gregory the Great, *Forty Gospel Homilies*, 1.

10. Gregory the Great, *Forty Gospel Homilies*, 212.

11. Gregory the Great, *Forty Gospel Homilies*, 212.

12. Gregory the Great, *Forty Gospel Homilies*, 212.

13. Gregory the Great, *Forty Gospel Homilies*, 212.

[*inimicum propter te*]."[14] Gregory shares Augustine's basic principle that God is to be loved for his own sake, and all other things either in God or for the sake of God. Both friend and enemy are thus ordered to the love of God. When we fail to order our loves properly, we experience disorder in our own soul, and this internal disorder is what characterizes us as sinners. Moreover, according to Gregory, if we fail to love our enemy properly, we actually create a new kind of "enemy," an internal enemy rooted within our passions:

> If we begin to hate our enemy, our loss is of something internal. When we suffer something external from a neighbor, we must be on our guard against a hidden ravager within. This one is never better overcome than when we love the one who ravages us from without.[15]

Hating one's enemy for attacking one's property disorders the soul, which is now "ravaged" within. Such hatred reveals a disordered love within the soul: one's love for material things has caused one to hate a person created in God's image. Loving one's enemy naturally counteracts this. The supreme example of this love, of course, is Christ: "This is why Truth himself bore the suffering of the cross and yet bestowed his love on his persecutors, saying: *Father, forgive them for they know not what they do.*"[16] With this text, Gregory subtly introduces a way of transforming an enemy into a friend:

> Why should we wonder that his living disciples loved their enemies, when their dying master loved his? He expressed the depth of his love when he said: *No one has greater love than this, that he lay down his life for his friends.* The Lord had come to die even for his enemies [*pro inimicis*], and yet he said he would lay down his life for his friends [*pro amicis*] to show us that when we are able to win over our enemies by loving them even our persecutors become our friends.[17]

14. Augustine, *Confessions*, 4.14.
15. Gregory the Great, *Forty Gospel Homilies*, 213.
16. Gregory the Great, *Forty Gospel Homilies*, 213.
17. Gregory the Great, *Forty Gospel Homilies*, 213.

Loving one's enemies for the sake of God, because Christ has commanded it, transforms enemies into friends. This love derives its transforming power from the sacrifice of Christ. Thus love for friends and love for enemies become one and the same thing.

The text "No one has greater love than this, that he lay down his life for his friends" is the central theme of the homily. The sacrificial love of Christ, which makes an enemy into a friend, raises the next question: what exactly does it mean to be a friend of Christ? Gregory begins to answer this question as he leads his audience through the remainder of the Gospel reading. Commenting on the text "You are my friends, if you do whatever I command you" (John 15:13), Gregory writes:

> How great is our Creator's mercy! We are unworthy servants, and he calls us friends. How great is our human value, that we should be friends of God [*amicos Dei*]! You've heard your glorious dignity—now listen to what the struggle costs. *If you do whatever I command you. You are my friends, if you do whatever I command you.*[18]

So what does friendship with God entail? Clearly it involves obedience to the commands of Jesus. Gregory further indicates that this friendship involves a struggle. He illustrates this by alluding to Jesus's response to the mother of James and John, who requested a "place of eminence" for each of her sons:

> They were seeking a place of eminence. Truth called them back to the way by which they could come to it, as if he were saying: "This place of eminence delights you now, but first you must follow the way of suffering [*via laboris*]. The cup is the way to greatness. If your heart is seeking what allures it, first drink what causes it pain. Only through the bitter drink which is prepared for it does it reach the joy of salvation."[19]

What is this *via laboris*, this "way of suffering"? The word *labor*, on its most basic level, means "toil" or "exertion," but it also can

---

18. Gregory the Great, *Forty Gospel Homilies*, 214.
19. Gregory the Great, *Forty Gospel Homilies*, 214.

convey the idea of hardship or distress. For Gregory, it signifies the active endurance of hardship characteristic of discipleship. To be a friend of God is to do as Jesus commands. He commands his friends to follow him in the way of active suffering, which involves self-denial and despising the things of the world. This *via laboris*, in keeping with the nature of Christian asceticism, is not suffering as an end in itself, but serves to free one from the preoccupation with temporal things and focus one's attention on things eternal. Thus, a true "friend of God" is one who is focused on eternal goods. Returning the Johannine text, "I have called you friends, because everything I have heard from my Father I have made known to you" (15:15), Gregory asks what these "things" Jesus has heard from the Father might be: "Are they not the festivals of our heavenly home which he daily impresses on our hearts by his inspiring love? . . . Transformed from their earthly desires, they were burning with flames of the supreme love."[20]

Having laid such heavy emphasis upon friendship with God, does Gregory give any real thought to human friendships? Unlike his predecessors—i.e., Augustine, Ambrose, Gregory Nazianzen, and, to a lesser extent, John Cassian—he does not engage the classical tradition of friendship in any significant way. Nevertheless, his idea of the friend of God does have a certain social application. We see this when he inserts a passage from the Psalms into the homily: "Your friends, O God, have become exceedingly honorable to me" (Psalm 139:17). Gregory then provides his own definition of a friend, one not drawn from the classical tradition: "A friend can be called a kind of soul-keeper [*animi custos*]."[21] What does it mean for one to "keep" or take care of the soul of another? It means providing a good example:

> Since the psalmist looked forward to seeing God's chosen ones separated from love of this world, and keeping his will by observing the divine mandates, he marveled

20. Gregory the Great, *Forty Gospel Homilies*, 214–15.

21. Gregory the Great, *Forty Gospel Homilies*, 215. The definition of friend as "soul-keeper" or "guardian of the spirit" is also found in Isidore of Seville, *Etymologies*, 10.4.

at God's friends, saying: *Your friends, O God, have be-come exceedingly honorable to me!* And as if he were immediately seeking to learn the reasons for such great honor, he adds: *Their pre-eminence has been exceedingly strengthened.* We see God's elect subduing their bodies, strengthening their spirits, commanding demons, shin-ing with virtues, despising things of this present life, preaching our eternal homeland by voice and character, loving it even when they are dying and attaining it by their sufferings.[22]

Here Gregory gives a brief litany of the life of Christian asceti-cism, undoubtedly drawn from his monastic formation and now applied to the lives of the faithful living in the world. Gregory ends his consideration of friendship with a suitable admonition: "But let one who has obtained the dignity of being called a friend of God observe that the gifts he perceives in himself are beyond him; let him attribute nothing to his own merits so that he become an enemy."[23] In his homily, Gregory exhorts the members of his audi-ence, lay and religious alike, to become friends of God and thus become soul-keeping friends of one another.

Anselm of Canterbury

The monastic idea of friendship finds keen expression in Anselm of Canterbury (ca. 1033–1109). Anselm is known for his many contributions to medieval, pre-scholastic philosophy and theol-ogy, representing one of the highest achievements of monastic thought. While Benedictine monasticism emphasized the cultiva-tion of those moral and spiritual virtues necessary for salvation, it also made provision for learning. Each monastery had a school to train oblates to read, with literacy serving two essential functions of reciting the divine office and private study. Monastic study cen-tered on *lectio divina*, the prayerful, meditative reading of sacred

22. Gregory the Great, *Forty Gospel Homilies*, 215.
23. Gregory the Great, *Forty Gospel Homilies*, 216.

Scripture and the church fathers.[24] To read effectively, however, the monks were to be trained in the seven liberal arts, which were divided into two sections: the *Trivium*, consisting of grammar, rhetoric, and logic; and the *Quadrivium*, comprised of mathematics, geometry, astronomy, and music. This curriculum enabled the gifted monk not only to study Scripture, but also to ruminate thoughtfully on theological and philosophical questions. Anselm was such a monk. He is an example of what might be called monastic erudition: the learned, eloquent exposition and development of theological and philosophical ideas nurtured by *lectio divina*. His "ontological argument" for the existence of God is debated in philosophy classes even today. The theory of the atonement set forth in his treatise *Cur Deus Homo* (*Why the God-Man*) still commands the respect of theologians. It is in his correspondence, however, that we encounter Anselm's understanding of friendship and the importance he placed on it. His letters, addressed primarily to brother monks or to those in some relation to the monastic community, present friendship as an essential part of religious life, a vital means whereby the soul may come to realize union with God. Richard Southern expresses the Anselmian ideal very well: "Total dedication to God, which for Anselm meant unalterable dedication to the monastic life, was the one requirement for complete acceptance in the community of friends."[25] It was toward union with God that Anselm's community of friends was directed.

Friendship for Anselm partakes of some of the basic qualities derived from the classical tradition. He employs the common idea of the friend as another self. In Anselm's thought, this idea signifies two monks so enjoined in the search for God that they identify with each other on the spiritual level, even after the death of one of the friends. He refers to a deceased monk named Osbern as "my other self" (*alteram meam*).[26] Elsewhere he writes of the same Osbern:

24. For an outstanding study of this tradition, see Robertson, *Lectio Divina*.
25. Southern, *Saint Anselm*, 147.
26. Anselm, *Letters*, 84.

> I ask you and all my friends to pray for the late Osbern, my sweetest friend [*dilectissimo meo*]. Wherever Osbern is, my soul is his soul [*anima eius anima mea est*]. May I therefore receive on his behalf, while living, what I could hope for from my friends when I am dead, so that they will be free of obligation to me when I die.[27]

We notice that Osbern and Anselm were so closely identified in life that now, in death, their souls are likewise identified: "my soul is his soul." Therefore, Anselm reasons, prayer for the soul of Osbern will redound to Anselm's own benefit even now. His close identification with his deceased friend draws his brother monks into a communion of prayer and intercession.

In addition to his use of the *topos* of the friend as another self, Anselm's understanding of the place of friendship in the spiritual life develops in two aspects: interiority and inexpressibility. We encounter the first in Anselm's letter to his friend Gundulf. Evidently, Gundulf and Anselm were dear friends separated by distance. In the letter, Anselm responds to Gundulf's disquiet at Anselm's lack of regular correspondence. He refers to Gundulf as "soul most beloved of my soul" (*anima dilectissima animae meae*), assuring him that their friendship, existing as it does on the spiritual level, transcends distance:

> For I see you as the sort of person I must love, as you know I do; I hear about you as the sort of person I must long for, as God knows I do. From this it comes about that wherever you may go my love follows you; and wherever I may be, my longing for you embraces you.[28]

Anselm's love for his friend is such that it follows him wherever he goes. Physical presence is irrelevant in such a relationship, existing as it does on the spiritual level. In this, we detect an echo of Cassian's emphasis upon unity of wills as opposed to unity of place. The strength of their friendship derives from its foundation:

---

27. Anselm, *Letters*, 82.
28. Anselm, *Letters*, 81.

the inner person. Specifically, the friendship is rooted in memory (*memoria*). Anselm writes:

> And do you inquire about me by your messengers, ex-
> hort me by your letters, shower me with your gifts that I
> may remember you? Let my tongue cleave fast to the roof
> of my mouth if I cease to remember you, if I do not place
> "Gundulf" at the pinnacle of my friendship [*in praecipuis
> amicitiae meae*]. I speak here not about Gundulf the lay-
> man, my father, but Gundulf the monk, our brother.
> How could I forget you? How could someone imprinted
> on my heart [*cordi meo imprimitur*] like a waxen seal slip
> out of my memory [*memoriae meae*]?[29]

Gundulf is "imprinted" on Anselm's memory "like a waxen seal." In antiquity and the Middle Ages, letters of import were sealed with wax which bore an image of some sort imprinted by a signet ring worn by the sender. This served both to identify the authen- ticity of the sender and to ensure confidentiality. In like manner, the "image" of Gundulf is imprinted in Anselm's memory; indeed, it is imprinted on his very heart. We remember that, for Cicero, a shared *memoria* served to console the surviving friends of one who had died, making it as though he were still among the living. In Anselm, *memoria* likewise serves to provide a sense of the pres- ence of an absent friend. The emphasis, however, is on interiority, in the inward nature of the memory. The memory of Gundulf is imprinted on Anselm's heart (*cordo*). This reflects the monastic, contemplative focus on the interior life of the soul. At the same time, the interiority is a shared interiority, evincing the intense interpersonal communion between the two persons:

> Even when you are silent I know you love me [*diligis me*];
> and if I am silent *you know that I love you* [*tu scis quia
> amo te*]. You are aware that I have no doubts about you,
> and I am your witness that you are sure of me. Since we
> are aware of each other's minds [*nostrarum conscientia-
> rium*], therefore, it only remains for us to tell each other

---

29. Anselm, *Letters*, 81.

about our affairs so that we may either rejoice together or
be concerned together.[30]

Two things in this passage reveal the intensely interpersonal as
well as theological dimension of Anselm's friendship with Gundulf. The first is Anselm's use of the word *conscientiarium*. It is
derived from *conscientia*, which can be translated as "mind," but
more specifically means "shared knowledge," and even a shared
moral awareness or "conscience." Thus each one knows the other
in the inner person, in the core of their being. Second, quoting the
Vulgate, Anselm employs the post-Resurrection conversation between Jesus and Peter from John 21. In the original context, Jesus
uses the phrase *diligis me* as a question: "Peter, do you love me?"
Peter, in turn, responds with *tu scis quia amo te*: "You know that I
love you."[31] Anselm transforms the significance of the passage so
that the question confirms the reality of their love. It is as if Anselm
is contrasting the relationship between Jesus and Peter, wounded
as it was by Peter's denial, with his relationship with Gundulf. Jesus
had to ask Peter if he loved him; Gundulf does not—or should
not—have to ask Anselm this question. Each knows the conscience
of the other, and thus each knows that the other loves him.

The other thing Anselm emphasizes in his understanding of
friendship is its inexpressibility. This is a natural corollary to interiority. Friendship resides in that place in the soul, the conscience,
where one is alone with God.[32] This proximity to the divine nature gives to monastic friendship the same apophatic nature that
characterizes contemplative theology.[33] Thus monastic friendship
is inexpressible. Anselm elucidates this in his letter to Haimo and

30. Anselm, *Letters*, 81.

31. John 21:15.

32. *Catechism of the Catholic Church*, para. 1776.

33. By "contemplative theology," I mean a theology rooted in contemplation, that is, the simple gazing of the mind upon God. As opposed to *kataphatic*
theology, i.e., theology that makes affirmative statements about God, contemplative theology prefers what is called the *apophatic* way: knowledge of God in
terms of what God is not. Since God must be experienced as opposed to being
cognitively understood, contemplative theology stresses intuition, feeling, and
self-abandonment in the belief that the divine essence is inexpressible.

Rainald, two of his kinsmen who arrived at Bec while Anselm was away on the affairs of the abbey, and whom he was trying to persuade to enter monastic life. He expresses his fervent desire in emotionally evocative language:

> When I heard, souls most beloved of my soul [*animae di-lectissimae animae meae*]—whom my soul loves as itself and for whom it desires what it desires for itself [*desid-erat anima mea*]—when I heard that you had come such a long distance to seek my face I cannot express what great joy flooded my heart, how much my hope for you increased, how high my already ardent longing for you flamed up, even intensely.[34]

Here again Anselm uses the same language he used in his letter to Gundulf: his kinsmen are "souls most beloved of [his] soul." This is his regular greeting for those whom he has befriended. In addition, we encounter here the language of desire being used in connection to friendship. In the monastic tradition, "desire" signifies what Dom Jean Leclercq has described as "an obscure possession, awareness of which does not last, and consequently gives rise to regret at seeing it disappear and a desire to find it again."[35] According to Leclercq, the monastic life is characterized, fundamentally, by the desire (*desideratus*) for God.[36] Monastic friendship partakes of this desire, a desire for a shared union with God. Since Haimo and Rainald are his close friends, what Anselm desires for his own soul (*desiderat anima mea*) he desires for them. He then tells them that he yearns ardently for their company, so that he may rejoice completely with them in the life to come.[37] "This," he writes, "the innermost depths of my heart choose for you, dearly beloved."[38] Anselm shares with Haimo and Rainald, his blood relations, the same intense, interior love he has with Gundulf. As he continues the letter, however, his language indicates an inability to adequate-

34. Anselm, *Letters*, 285.
35. Leclercq, *Love of Learning*, 30.
36. This, of course, is the theme of Leclercq's book.
37. Anselm, *Letters*, 285.
38. Anselm, *Letters*, 285–86.

ly express this love: "But why do I hesitate openly to express the desire of my heart? I may speak, but let God persuade."[39] He then gives an emotionally evocative entreaty for them to join him in the monastic vocation:

> My longed-for friends [*desiderati mei*], you can do nothing so good as to grasp the intention of the monastic life. Nowhere can you do this better than with him who desires [*desiderat*] this for you and who can, God granting, serve and advise you. In any case, I do not deceive you, because I am your friend [*amicus*] and certainly I am not deceived, for I have experienced it. Let us, therefore, be monks together, let us serve God together, so that we may rejoice together over each other now and in the future. We are one flesh and one blood [*unus caro, unus sanguis*]; let us be one soul and one spirit [*una anima, unus spiritus*].[40]

Here again Anselm uses the language of desire to convey his sense of friendship. He refers to his friends as *desiderati mei*, literally "my desired ones." The closer the friendship between brother monks—or, in this case, potential monks—the more the relationship takes on the characteristics of desire. There is also a longing for their presence, reflecting the longing for God's presence. Anselm exhorts them to the "intention of the monastic life," and uses their friendship as the setting in which to realize this intention. Nowhere can Haimo and Rainald better succeed at the monastic vocation than with one who is their "friend" (*amicus*), and who "desires" (*desiderat*) this for them. He therefore urges that they be monks together, and that their oneness in flesh (*caro*) and blood (*sanguis*) be supplemented, and even superseded by, a oneness in soul (*anima*) and spirit (*spiritus*). He continues by emphasizing that this desire of his, which they themselves have awakened by coming to Bec, has made their friendship truly indissoluble:

> Moreover, you have approached, by approaching you have enkindled [*conflastis*] the fire, by enkindling

39. Anselm, *Letters*, 286.
40. Anselm, *Letters*, 286.

[*conflando*] the fire you burst into flame, by bursting into
flame you fused my soul with your souls. It can be torn
away but it can no longer be separated.[41]

Anselm's desire for Haimo and Rainald's vocation, which he
describes as a fire which they have "enkindled" (*conflastis*), has
"fused" their souls with his. They are now friends joined in the
heart, the seat of the affections. This same desire, this affection, is
inexpressible: "O, how my love burns within my heart; how all my
affection strives to break out at once! How it seeks to express itself
in words but no words suffice; how much it wants to disclose itself,
but neither time nor parchment can contain it."[42] Again, Anselm's
love for his friends has so intensified at the prospect of their becoming monks that it cannot be expressed in language. Anselm
therefore appeals to Christ to persuade them in the interior sanc-
tuary of their hearts, to speak to them on a level beyond words:

> O, speak to their hearts, good Jesus; without you no voice
> can prevail on their ears. Tell them to give up everything
> and follow you. Promise them that when you come to
> judge, they will sit with you and judge with you. Do not
> separate from me those whom you have joined to me by
> such affection of flesh and spirit, but gather them up with
> those serving you, whom you commanded me to serve.
> Lord, you are my witness within [*testis interius*], and the
> tears I shed while writing this are my outward witnesses
> [*testes exterius*] to how much my heart would rejoice if
> they were to enter the monastery with me.[43]

Anselm prays that Jesus will persuade his kinsmen on the inner,
affective, inexpressible level. Likewise, he appeals to interiority as
proof of his love for them. Jesus is the *testis interius*, literally "interior witness," who confirms Anselm's inexpressible love for Haimo
and Rainald. At the same time, there is an external confirmation
as well: Anselm's tears. These are his *testes exterius*, literally his

---

41. Anselm, *Letters*, 286.

42. Anselm, *Letters*, 287.

43. Anselm, *Letters*, 287.

"external witnesses," testifying to the veracity of his love in non-verbal, affective action.

We again encounter this external, nonverbal expression of the inward reality of love in Anselm's letter to Gilbert, Abbot of Westminster. Saluting the abbot as "friend, brother, fellow-monk, father, beloved friend," Anselm begins by acknowledging the inability of language to convey accurately the reality of their friendship: "If I wished to write about the affection of our mutual love I would be afraid of appearing to those ignorant of it to overstep the truth, or of being forced to detract something from the truth."[44] Anselm fears exaggeration or understatement if he attempts to express their friendship in words. He then appeals to affective action:

> Since, therefore, it is not possible to express adequately in writing what we mean to each other, and since I am not speaking to someone who is ignorant of this, leaving all this aside for the moment, I pray with you that when we see each other again we should once more revive face to face [*oculo ad oculum*], lip to lip [*ocsulo ad osculum*], embrace to embrace [*amplexu ad amplexum*], our unforgotten love.[45]

The love of their friendship, inexpressible in words, finds expression in outward actions of affection: "face to face" (*oculo ad oculum*, literally, "eye to eye"), "lip to lip," "embrace to embrace."[46] The love between friends within the monastic milieu is profoundly interior and thus cannot be comprehended by human language. Nonetheless, the body itself contains its own language, and since monastic observance involves both the inward disposition as well as outward deportment, we would expect monastic friendship to find expression in bodily actions.

44. Anselm, *Letters*, 305.

45. Anselm, *Letters*, 305.

46. The phrase "lip to lip" refers to the customary kiss one would give to another as an outward sign of inward affection; it does not suggest anything sexual.

Aelred of Rievaulx

It is clear from our exploration of the *Rule* of Benedict and Anselm's letters that interpersonal communion and friendship together constituted a dynamic force in monastic life. We see this
idea fully developed in Aelred of Rievaulx (1110–1167). Aelred
was part of the Cistercian reform movement, which sought to
return Benedictine monasticism to the original simplicity of the
Rule. Benedictine monasteries had largely become quite wealthy in
the intervening years between the time of Benedict and the twelfth
century, characterized by magnificent chapels, ornate liturgical
vessels, elaborate liturgies, and near-abandonment of manual
labor, the vast monastic estates being cultivated by serfs. The Cis-
tercians sought a return to corporate poverty, manual labor, and
simplified liturgy.[47] However, learning (which occupied a central
role in Benedictine life) continued. Aelred was himself a product
of this, another example of monastic erudition. His work *Spiritual
Friendship* is an explicitly Christian appropriation of Cicero's *De
Amicitia*. Like *De Amicitia*, it is written in the form of a dialogue.
In this work, Aelred engages several of his fellow monks in an ex-
tensive discussion on Cicero's doctrine in light of sacred Scripture.
He states his specific goal in the person of Ivo, a young novice:

> I want to be more fully taught about the right kind of
> friendship between us, which should begin in Christ [*in
> Christo inchoetur*], be maintained according Christ [*et
> secundum Christum servetur*], and have its end and value
> referred to Christ [*et ad Christum finis eius et utilitas
> referatur*]. It is obvious indeed that Cicero was ignorant
> of the virtue of true friendship, since he was completely
> ignorant of Christ, who is the beginning and end of
> friendship.[48]

In this passage we notice that Christ is definitive for authentic
friendship. Friendship begins "in Christ," is "maintained according to Christ," and is ultimately "referred to Christ." This might be

47. Lawrence, *Medieval Monasticism*, 173.

48. Aelred, *Spiritual Friendship*, 1.8.

called the christogenic quality of friendship, a quality that defines the very nature of friendship as a virtue that forms the character of the person. And while, in Aelred's view, Cicero was ignorant of this the true essence of friendship, Aelred uses Cicero's own definition as his point of departure: "friendship is agreement [*consensio*] in things human and divine, with goodwill and charity [*benevolentia et caritate*]."[49] For the ancient Romans, including Cicero, *caritas* meant "esteem" or "affection."[50] In the Christian tradition, *caritas* came to signify love of God for his own sake and love of neighbor for the sake of God, i.e., a theological virtue, given by the Holy Spirit at baptism, not rooted in human nature and thus not obtainable by human effort. Given this new understanding of *caritas*, the question then, is this: must one be a Christian in order to have true friendship? Again speaking through Ivo, Aelred puts the question this way: "I admit that for me this definition would be satisfying enough, if I did not suspect that it suited not only pagans and Jews but also unjust Christians. I also admit my conviction that true friendship cannot exist between those who live without Christ."[51] The question raised by Aelred goes beyond what Christianity may add to friendship or how the Greco-Roman understanding of friendship is transformed by Christianity. Aelred's thesis is that true friendship is rooted in Christ, and therefore is only possible among those devoted to Christ. Indeed, Aelred points to the first community of Christians in the Book of Acts as an example of genuine friendship as Cicero defined it:

> According to Cicero's definition, you would agree that those people excelled in the virtue of true friendship of whom it was said that "the multitude of believers was of one heart and one soul. No one claimed any belonging as his or her own, but all was held in common." How could the highest agreement in things divine and human, with

49. Aelred, *Spiritual Friendship*, 1.11.

50. See Cicero's definition in the first chapter: "Friendship [*amicitia*] is nothing else than an accord [*consensio*] in all things, human and divine, conjoined with mutual goodwill [*benevolentia*] and affection [*caritate*]."

51. Aelred, *Spiritual Friendship*, 1.16.

charity and goodwill, fail to exist among those who were
of one heart and soul? How many martyrs laid down
their lives for the brethren? How many spared neither
cost nor toil nor their bodies' torture?[52]

Continuing in the tradition of friendship bequeathed by the New
Testament and the church fathers, Aelred reinforces his view with
a quote from Jesus's Farewell Discourse: "No one has greater love
than to lay down his life for his friends."[53] The essence of friendship, for Aelred, is exemplified in *agape*, whereby one loves to the
point of making the ultimate sacrifice.

At this point in the text, the objection is raised that there is no
distinction between charity and friendship. Aelred distinguishes
between the two according to their respective recipients. We are
commanded to extend charity to all people, including our friends
as well as our enemies.[54] Friendship, however, is extended only to
those "to whom we have no qualm about entrusting our heart and
all its contents, while those friends are bound to us in turn by the
same inviolable law of loyalty and trustworthiness."[55] Does this
mean there are two kinds of charity, one for all people and another
for friends? By no means. For Aelred, friendship perfects charity,
i.e., it is the means whereby charity bears fruit. We see this in the
role friendship plays in the spiritual development of the Christian.
"Friendship," writes Aelred, "bears fruit in our present life and in
the next."[56] In terms of this life, friendship "is a foundation for all
the virtues, with its virtue it destroys the vices."[57] Aelred continues:

> Friendship so cushions adversity and chastens prosperity
> that among mortals almost nothing can be enjoyed with-
> out a friend. A friendless person is like an animal, having
> no one in whom to rejoice in prosperity and grieve in
> sadness, in whom to confide if the mind suspects some

52. Aelred, *Spiritual Friendship*, 1.28.
53. Aelred, *Spiritual Friendship*, 1.30.
54. Aelred, *Spiritual Friendship*, 1.32.
55. Aelred, *Spiritual Friendship*, 1.32.
56. Aelred, *Spiritual Friendship*, 2.9.
57. Aelred, *Spiritual Friendship*, 2.10.

> threat and with whom to communicate an unusually
> sublime or splendid event . . . But how happy, how care-
> free, how joyful you are if you have a friend with whom
> you may talk as freely as with yourself, to whom you
> neither fear to confess any fault nor blush at revealing
> any spiritual progress, to whom you may entrust all the
> secrets of your heart and confide all your plans.[58]

Here again we have an allusion to a friend as another self, one in
whom one can confide one's innermost secrets without fear of
betrayal. It is this intimacy, this relationship with the other self,
that enables friendship to become the avenue of spiritual growth
and life with God. Friendship is the highest of stages leading to
perfection.[59] Aelred writes:

> Friendship is a stage bordering upon that perfection
> which consists in the love and knowledge of God, so
> that man from being a friend of his fellow man becomes
> the friend of God, according to the words of the Savior
> in the Gospel: "I will not now call you servants, but my
> friends."[60]

Again, Aelred alludes to the Farewell Discourse in the Gospel of
John. Friendship between Christians is a virtue that habituates
one for friendship with Christ. How does friendship accomplish
this? Within the dynamic of Christian friendship, all of the natural
goods of friendship are gradually purified and come to perfection
in Christ: "In friendship, then, we join honesty with kindness,
truth with joy, sweetness with goodwill, and affection with kind
action. All this begins with Christ, is advanced through Christ, and
is perfected in Christ [*in Christo perficiuntur*]."[61] Aelred continues:

> The ascent does not seem too steep or too unnatural,
> then, from Christ inspiring the love with which we love
> a friend to Christ's offering himself to us as the friend
> we may love, so that tenderness may yield to tenderness,

58. Aelred, *Spiritual Friendship*, 2.11.
59. Aelred, *Spiritual Friendship*, 2.15.
60. Aelred, *Spiritual Friendship*, 2.14.
61. Aelred, *Spiritual Friendship*, 2.20.

sweetness to sweetness, and affection to affection. Hence a friend clinging to a friend in the spirit of Christ [*in spiritu Christi*] becomes one heart [*cor unum*] and one soul [*anima una*] with him. Thus mounting the steps of love to the friendship of Christ, a friend becomes one with him in the kiss of the spirit. Sighing for the kiss, one holy soul cried out, "let him kiss me with the kiss of his mouth!"[62]

Yet again we have a very subtle but real allusion to the friend as another self. As one clings to one's friend in Christ, one becomes "one heart [*cor unum*] and one soul [*anima una*]" with Christ. This is "friendship with Christ," in that we could say that Christ has become another self, one in whom one can confide any secret, share any joy, and commiserate in any sorrow. Also, Aelred alludes to the opening verse of the Song of Songs: "Let him kiss me with the kiss of his mouth." Medieval commentators viewed this as the experience of the soul in the spiritual embrace of Christ. Thus, in true friendship, each person becomes the intensely personal means for the other to befriend Christ. In fact, Christ comes to the soul in and through the person of the friend, a meeting which Aelred describes in terms of a "kiss." Drawing upon the tradition of the spiritual interpretation of sacred Scripture, where something has both a literal meaning as well as a spiritual significance, Aelred sees in the phenomenon of a kiss (*osculum*) a twofold meaning, one physical and one spiritual: "Let us consider the characteristics of this kiss of the flesh, that from what is of the flesh we may rise to the spirit, from what is human to the divine."[63] In a kiss between two persons, "two spirits meet, blend, and unite."[64] This coming together of two spirits awakens affection within the two persons.[65]

62. Aelred, *Spiritual Friendship*, 2.20–21.

63. Aelred, *Spiritual Friendship*, 2.22.

64. Aelred, *Spiritual Friendship*, 2.23.

65. Aelred clearly understands what we all experience when we kiss anyone for whom we have any level of emotional feeling, e.g., a brother, a sister, a parent, a child. What strikes us as odd is Aelred's emphasis upon the joining of lips, but this, I think, is more of a cultural estrangement than anything else. In the ancient and medieval worlds, a kiss on the lips was a standard, non-erotic

We notice that the physical kiss is a means of ascent to the spiritual. How does this ascent occur? What are its implications for friendship? Aelred discusses three kisses in succession: the physical kiss, the spiritual kiss, and the intellectual kiss:

> So there exist physical kisses [*osculum corporale*], spiritual kisses [*osculum spiritale*], and intellectual kisses [*osculum intellectuale*]. The physical kiss is made with the imprint of the lips, the spiritual kiss with the joining of spirits, and the intellectual kiss with the infusion of grace by the spirit of God.[66]

The physical kiss serves as a sign of reconciliation between those who previously had been enemies, as a sign of peace between those in church, as a sign of love between a husband and wife, as a sign of affection between friends, and as a sign of Catholic unity.[67] From this, Aelred proceeds to a description of the spiritual kiss. While the physical kiss is shared among all to whom we are bound by charity, the spiritual kiss, while partaking of charity, is shared only among friends. Here is where the actual ascent to God begins:

> Now the spiritual kiss belongs to friends who are bound by the one law of friendship [*una amicitiae lege*]. This takes place not through a touch of the mouth but through the attachment of the mind, not by joining lips but by blending spirits, while the Spirit of God purifies all things and by sharing himself pours in a heavenly flavor. This kiss I would aptly name the kiss of Christ [*osculum Christi*], which he offers, however, through the lips of another, not his own. He inspires in friends that most holy affection, so that to them it seems that there exists but one soul in different bodies, and so they may say with the prophet, *see how good and how pleasant it is for brethren to live in unity.*[68]

greeting, even—and especially—between individuals of the same sex and close relatives.

66. Aelred, *Spiritual Friendship*, 2.24.

67. Aelred, *Spiritual Friendship*, 2.24.

68. Aelred, *Spiritual Friendship*, 2.26.

The mutual goods shared between friends, i.e., confidence, common interests, goodwill, affection, are all signified by a kiss and come from Christ through the person of one's friend. Friendship thus takes on a certain sacramental quality in that it is a natural thing that becomes a means of grace and ascent to God. We see this in the "intellectual kiss." The spiritual kiss of friendship evokes a longing for what lies beyond, for the direct, incomprehensible love of Christ:

> Having grown accustomed to this kiss and confident that all this sweetness derives from Christ . . . the soul sighs for that intellectual [*intellectuale*] kiss and cries with deepest yearning, "let him kiss me with the kiss of his mouth." So at last, with earthly attachments calmed and all worldly thoughts and desires lulled, it may delight in the kiss of Christ alone [*solius Christi osculo*] and rest in his embrace.[69]

Medieval theologians and philosophers used the word *intellectus* to denote the human mind or intellect. Intellect is the seat of reason, and reason is the basis for the image of God in the human person. Therefore, the soul experiences its greatest intimacy with God in the *intellectus*. For Aelred, the *intellectus* becomes the locus of the "kiss of Christ alone," where the soul experiences the most intimate relationship with Christ. In this way, friendship becomes a means of ascent to union with God. It is not that friendship goes beyond charity; charity (*caritas*) is an integral part of friendship, and friendship becomes the means of fully realizing the fruits of charity.

Thomas Aquinas

We turn now to Thomas Aquinas (1225–1274). In the twelfth and thirteenth centuries, the locus of intellectual activity gradually shifted from the monastery to the university. Along with this transition, there was a move away from the *lectio divina* of

---

69. Aelred, *Spiritual Friendship*, 2.27.

the monasteries to a more academic, philosophical approach to theology. This new approach came to be known as scholasticism. Scholasticism was characterized by an orderly, dialogical approach to a given topic, beginning with the *quaestio*, which was essentially a way of introducing a topic for investigation in the form of an inquiry or "question." While the form varied somewhat depending on the individual, typically the *quaestio* began with the positing of a question, e.g., whether God exists. The theologian then followed with a series of arguments for the contrary position, called "objections," drawn from sacred Scripture, church tradition, and various ancient and medieval authorities. Then, he would present his own position in form of an affirmation, e.g., "I answer that," followed by a series of arguments defending his own position, also supported by Scripture, dogmatic tradition, and philosophy. Finally, he would answer and refute the opposing objections. It was a very tightly argued way of arriving at the truth of a theological problem. Moreover, the emergence of scholasticism coincided with the rediscovery of Aristotle's philosophical body of works. Most of Aristotle's writings, with the exception of his treatises on logic, were unknown in the West until the thirteenth century, when Latin translations of his *Metaphysics, On the Soul, Nichomachean Ethics*, and other works became available, largely based upon Arabic translations of the original Greek texts.[70] For the first time, Christian thinkers had access to a pre-Christian authority who was not only a profound thinker, but also "the expounder of a comprehensive system."[71] Thomas Aquinas, who was a teacher of theology at the University of Paris, studied Aristotle assiduously and incorporated the best of Aristotle's thought into a comprehensive theological system, the *Summa Theologiae*.

It is in the *Summa* that Thomas discusses the nature of friendship. Relying heavily on Aristotle's treatment in *Nichomachean Ethics* and Augustine's *Confessions*, Thomas reiterates some of the traditional ideas of friendship, specifically that friendship

---

70. Copleston, *History of Medieval Philosophy*, 154.
71. Copleston, *History of Medieval Philosophy*, 155.

is a habit,[72] and that the friend is another self.[73] What is the most developed in Thomas's treatment of friendship is his understanding of friendship in relation to charity. Before he explores this, he presents a thorough exposition of the basic meaning of love (*amor*). According to Thomas, love is rooted in appetite. By "appetite" he means the capacity for being moved toward a desirable object. Love (*amor*) signifies the movement of the soul toward the beloved object, a movement which the appetitive faculty of the soul makes possible.[74] This movement ensues from an apprehension of a beloved object within the intellect, evoking a movement of the will.[75] The beloved object affects a change in the soul when the soul apprehends the beloved. This change, operative in the will, is called "love" (*amor*).[76] Having defined love as a movement of the will, Thomas then distinguishes two particular types of love: "love of concupiscence" (*amor concupiscentiae*) and "love of friendship" (*amor amicitiae*).[77] In this distinction, we begin to see Thomas's understanding of friendship as directed to the other for the sake of the other. Drawing upon Aristotle, Thomas writes:

> As the Philosopher says (Rhet. ii, 4), "to love is to wish good to someone." Hence the movement of love has a twofold tendency: towards the good which a man wishes to someone (to himself or to another) and towards that to which he wishes some good. Accordingly, a man has love of concupiscence towards the good that he wishes another, and love of friendship towards him to whom he wishes good.[78]

In other words, love of concupiscence or desire is a love directed toward a lovable object that one desires for enjoyment, either

72. Aquinas, *Summa Theologiae*, 2.1.26.3.

73. Aquinas, *Summa Theologiae*, 2.1.28.2.

74. Aquinas, *Summa Theologiae*, 2.1.26.1.

75. Aquinas, *Summa Theologiae*, 2.1.26.1.

76. Aquinas, *Summa Theologiae*, 2.1.26.2.

77. The word *concupiscentia* for Thomas means simply "desire" or "longing" and does not necessarily imply a disordered desire.

78. Aquinas, *Summa Theologiae*, 2.1.26.4.

for oneself or for another. Thus, it is not necessarily a selfish desire. Still, love of friendship is qualitatively different. While love of concupiscence is directed to the good object that one desires one's friend to enjoy (and perhaps to enjoy with the friend), love of friendship is directed to the actual person. It is directed, not to the good one wishes to one's friend, but to the good inherent in the friend. In fact, insofar as friendship partakes of concupiscence, it "loses the character of true friendship."[79]

If *amor amicitiae*, the love of friendship, is inherently other-directed, then it bears a very close similarity to charity. Accordingly, Thomas addresses the question of whether charity is friendship. He gives a prelude to his answer when he briefly discusses zeal in relation to love. The contrary position in the *Summa* is that zeal is inherently opposed to love: "zeal is the beginning of contention . . . but contention is incompatible with love."[80] Thomas answers that "zeal, whatever way we take it, arises from the intensity of love."[81] He continues as follows:

> For it is evident that the more intensely a power tends to anything, the more vigorously it withstands opposition or resistance. Since therefore love is "a movement toward a beloved object," as Augustine says (QQ. 83, qu. 35), an intense love seeks to remove everything that opposes it.[82]

For Thomas, zeal naturally ensues from intense love. It can emerge from love of concupiscence, when one desires an object so intensely that one is moved against all who hinder the gaining or enjoyment of the object.[83] Zeal can also emerge from love of friendship when it causes one to be moved against all that is opposed to the

---

79. Aquinas, *Summa Theologiae*, 2.1.26.4.

80. Aquinas, *Summa Theologiae*, 2.1.28.4.

81. Aquinas, *Summa Theologiae*, 2.1.28.4.

82. Aquinas, *Summa Theologiae*, 2.1.28.4.

83. Aquinas, *Summa Theologiae*, 2.1.28.4.

good of one's friend.[84] Furthermore, this zeal can emerge from the love of God:

> In this way, too, a man is said to be zealous on God's behalf, when he endeavors, to the best of his means, to repel whatever is contrary to the honor or will of God; according to 1 Kings 19:14: "With zeal I have been zealous for the Lord of hosts." Again on the words of John 2:17: "The zeal of Thy house hath eaten me up."[85]

This implies that there is a friendship for God, a love for another for the sake of the other; in this case, a love for God for God's own sake, a love that gives rise to a zealous movement of the soul against anything opposed to the good of the divine friend. Thus, friendship, when directed toward God, seems to be identical with charity.

From here, Thomas directly addresses the question of whether friendship is the same as charity. The contrary position to this is that charity is not friendship. The main objection argues from the distinction between the two that we find in Aelred, that "by charity we love even sinners, whereas friendship based upon the virtuous is only for virtuous men."[86] In his response, Thomas quotes the Gospel of John: "On the contrary, it is written (John 15:15): 'I will not now call you servants . . . but My friends.' Now this was said to them by reason of nothing else than charity. Therefore charity is friendship."[87] He then alludes to Aristotle: "not every love has the character of friendship, but that love which is together with benevolence, when, to wit, we love someone so as to wish good to him."[88] This benevolence must be mutual, of course, for it to qualify as friendship, and this mutual benevolence entails "some kind of communication."[89] Thomas continues:

84. Aquinas, *Summa Theologiae*, 2.1.28.4.

85. Aquinas, *Summa Theologiae*, 2.1.28.4.

86. Aquinas, *Summa Theologiae*, 2.2.23.3.

87. Aquinas, *Summa Theologiae*, 2.2.23.3.

88. Aquinas, *Summa Theologiae*, 2.2.23.3.

89. Aquinas, *Summa Theologiae*, 2.2.23.3.

> Since there is a communication between man and God, inasmuch as He communicates His happiness to us, some kind of friendship must needs be based on this same communication, of which it is written (1 Corinthians 1:9): "God is faithful: by Whom you are called into the fellowship of His Son." The love which is based upon this communication, is charity: wherefore it is evident that charity is the friendship of man for God.[90]

This mutual communication, which Thomas calls "fellowship," is the essence of friendship. The purest type of this communication is that between God and man, which is synonymous with charity. Therefore, reasons Thomas, charity is friendship in its purest form. What then of the distinction between charity and friendship which we find in Aelred? Thomas addresses this in his reply to Objection 2:

> Friendship extends to a person in two ways: first, in respect of himself, and in this way friendship never extends but to one's friends: secondly, it extends to someone in respect of another, as, when a man has friendship for a certain person, for his sake he loves all belonging to them, be they children, servants, or connected with him in any way. Indeed so much do we love our friends, that for their sake we love all who belong to them, even if they hurt or hate us; so that, in this way, the friendship of charity extends even to our enemies, whom we love out of charity in relation to God, to whom the friendship of charity is chiefly directed.[91]

In the first instance, friendship adheres to the classical distinction in which it includes only those who reciprocate our good will and share our common interests. In the second instance, however—and this idea seems to be particular to Thomas Aquinas—this same good will toward our friend is extended to those whom our friend loves, even if those others happen to be our own enemies. The basis of this extension is my friendship with God, who loves

90. Aquinas, *Summa Theologiae*, 2.2.23.3.
91. Aquinas, *Summa Theologiae*, 2.2.23.3.

all people, including my enemies. Charity (love for God for his own sake) becomes the conduit whereby friendship is extended universally.

What then becomes of the mutuality inherent in friendship? At first glance, it appears that Thomas has compromised the classical understanding of friendship by extending it to those who do not reciprocate our good will. If reciprocity is lost, then isn't friendship, as a distinct form of charity, also lost? I can certainly love my enemy; indeed, I am obligated to do so. But I cannot truly be a friend to my enemy, for the terms are mutually contradictory. However, while reciprocity is part of friendship, all of the authors we have examined agree that the most important element of friendship is charity, which is taken to mean benevolence, i.e., wishing good for the other for the sake of the other. Charity in its truest sense, however, must be understood theologically. It is love for God for his own sake and my neighbor for the sake of God. This "for the sake of God" is, paradoxically, for the very sake of the neighbor as well, for his or her true and lasting good is found only in God. To love my neighbor for his or her own sake is to direct them to God. Now if charity thus understood is all inclusive by nature, and if charity is the heart of true friendship, then for friendship to fully realize itself it must be all-inclusive as well, extended even to those who do not presently reciprocate our good will. When we consider the matter from a theological/Thomistic perspective, reciprocity, while part of friendship, need not be actual; it can be potential. In other words, I must see my enemy as a potential friend. Herein we see the fullest restoration of the human person as the image of God. His capacity for interpersonal communion is extended even to his enemies, despite their ill will towards him, on account of this communion being rooted in a covenant relationship with God who befriended us, reconciling us to himself in Christ Jesus "while we were enemies" (Rom 5:10).

Conclusion

In the Middle Ages, we see remarkable development of the concept of friendship. As in Christian antiquity, so in the Middle Ages the classical understanding of friendship continued to be used, albeit transformed, by the fathers of the church. Many of the writers we examine allude to the friend as another self. Gregory reiterates the Augustinian principle that one is to love one's friend "in God" and one's enemy "for the sake of God." Also with Gregory we see the ongoing monastic influence that began with John Cassian. Friendship takes its place within the monastic regimen and becomes oriented toward the union of the soul with God. The ascetical life focuses the soul upon God and at the same time makes the soul solicitous for the spiritual welfare of one's neighbor. Thus, Gregory conceives of a friend as a "soul-keeper." Anselm continues in this vein and underscores the interiority and inexpressibility of friendship, these by virtue of the relationship's proximity to the divine nature. Aelred makes friendship the preferred venue for the spiritual life of the monk. He stresses that friendship begins in Christ, is maintained through Christ, and is perfected in Christ. The love of a friend becomes the means of experiencing the love of Christ, thus giving human friendship a certain sacramental quality. In this way, Aelred synthesizes the Ciceronian ideal with Christian revelation, bringing monastic friendship to its apogee. Finally, in Thomas Aquinas we see a further development of the relation between friendship and charity, culminating in the discovery that charity actually *is* friendship. Friendship with God—which is the essence of charity, according to the Gospel of John—requires that I love what my friend God loves, which includes even my enemies. Thus, Thomas brings the Augustinian principle of friendship to the fore. Friendship comes to its full realization only when it is universalized in charity.

4

Friendship in the Renaissance

IN THE MIDDLE AGES, friendship was seen as a means, for some even the preferred means, of achieving Christian perfection. For Aelred, friendship begins in Christ, continues in Christ, and is perfected in Christ. For Thomas Aquinas, friendship is universalized in charity. We see similar strains of thought in the Renaissance. The Renaissance is the name given to that period in European history that witnessed the rebirth of classical forms and ideals in art, literature, architecture, and sociopolitical life. This movement toward the recovery of classical culture describes a term that has become synonymous with the Renaissance: humanism. Humanism is the name given by later historians to the intellectual, literary, and artistic sensibilities that dominated the culture of the fourteenth, fifteenth, and sixteenth centuries. In simplest terms, Renaissance humanism consisted of three things: a recovery of classical styles in art, i.e., realism and perspective; a turn away from medieval scholastic philosophy toward literary studies; and a recovery of ancient texts in their original languages. The humanists of the Renaissance shared a universal contempt for medieval scholastic philosophy and theology. The humanist scorn for scholasticism was not so much a rejection of doctrine as a criticism of scholastic method. Late scholasticism, which dominated the universities in the fourteenth century, was characterized by abstract philosophical questions, by a preoccupation with overly subtle distinctions of logic, and by an ignorance of the historical and literary contexts of the texts the scholastic thinkers claimed to have mastered. In response, the humanists returned to the texts of antiquity, texts that provided both form and content for an educational program that they called "liberal studies," a program geared to the forming of character. Pietro Paolo Vergerio (1370–1444/45) expresses it well:

> We call those studies liberal which are worthy of a free man; those studies by which we attain and practice virtue and wisdom; that education which calls forth, trains, and develops those highest gifts of the body and mind which ennoble men and which are rightly judged to rank next in dignity to virtue only.[1]

It was this ethical pedagogical goal of "ennobling" the student which earned the name "humanist" for these thinkers.

Petrarch

Francesco Petrarch (1304–1374) is today considered the "father of humanism." As a young man, Petrarch undertook a legal career, but soon left the study of law in order to pursue literary studies. He is most remembered today for his letters. Renaissance humanism produced a widespread affinity for cultured correspondence between men-of-letters, and letter-writing became a way of establishing the interpersonal knowledge and communion characteristic of friendship. In his preface to his collection of letters, addressed to a friend under the name "Socrates," Petrarch gives advice on letter-writing. He says that one must adapt one's style and content to the nature of the recipient:

> We address a strong man in one way and weak one in another. The inexperienced youth and the old man who has fulfilled the duties of life, he who is puffed up with prosperity and he who is stricken with adversity, the scholar distinguished in literature and the man incapable

---

1. Vergerius, "De Ingenuis Moribus," 102.

of grasping anything beyond the commonplace,—each
must be treated according to his character or position.[2]

From this we can infer that letter-writing, while not necessarily
illustrative of genuine friendship, forces one to become knowledgeable of the various characters and circumstances of one's acquaintances. For Petrarch, letter-writing becomes "a simple matter
if we know the character of our correspondent and get used to his
particular mind."[3] Letter-writing thus facilitates genuine interpersonal communion.

What occasioned Petrarch's letter-writing was his discovery
of a manuscript in Verona containing a collection of letters written
by Cicero.[4] Barbara Caine expresses well the significance of the
discovery for the Renaissance idea of friendship: "Petrarch had not
come across this particular set of letters before. He seized on them
as providing an image of the 'real' Cicero, not a statesman or orator, but someone with whom he could be on intimate terms," going
so far as to address a letter to Cicero himself.[5] He then addressed
similar letters to his own like-minded friends.[6] His collection
includes letters written to his contemporary associates as well as
ancient writers long dead. In Petrarch's letters, we catch a glimpse
of his conception of friendship. Specifically, his letters exemplify
interpersonal communion. In the classical ideal, such communion
centered on like character and shared interests, particularly intellectual interests. For Renaissance humanists, one of these shared
interests was delight in good literature, characterized by artful,
polished rhetoric. For Petrarch, however, the relationship between
friendship and literary delight is more nuanced. While a delight
in the writing style of one's correspondent certainly is conducive
to friendship, at the same time friendship itself nurtures delight in
the style of the letter-writer. In the preface, we get a sense of the
relationship between affection and appreciation of literary style:

2. Petrarch, "To Socrates," 139.

3. Petrarch, "To Socrates," 137.

4. Caine, *Friendship*, 104.

5. Caine, *Friendship*, 105.

6. Caine, *Friendship*, 105.

> You, at least, will read the letters, my good Socrates, and, as you are very fond of your friends, you may discover some charm in them. Your partiality for the author will make his style pleasing (indeed what beauty of style is likely to be perceived by an unfriendly judge?); it is vain to adorn what already delights. If anything gratifies you in these letters of mine, I freely concede that it is not really mine but yours; that is to say, the credit is due not to my ability but to your good-will.[7]

For Petrarch, friendship is not only enhanced by literary delight; it also bestows this delight. Literary delight and affection mutually condition one another in an ever-deepening experience of interpersonal communion.

We sense this interpersonal communion, this intimate personal knowledge of the other, in two of Petrarch's letters. In his first letter to Cicero, Petrarch assumes a tone of familiarity and frankness that would suggest he knew Cicero personally (if we did not know better). He relates to Cicero his joy in having discovered his correspondence, and his delight when reading the letters: "At once I read them, over and over, with the utmost eagerness. And as I read I seemed to hear your bodily voice, O Marcus Tullius."[8] Petrarch then undertakes a lengthy chastisement of Cicero for allowing himself to be caught up in the political intrigues of the later Roman republic, which ultimately led to his death:

> Hearken, wherever you are, to the words of advice, or rather of sorrow and regret, that fall, not unaccompanied by tears, from the lips of one of your successors, who loves you faithfully and cherishes your name. O spirit ever restless and perturbed! In old age—I am but using your own words—self-involved in calamities and ruin! What good could you think would come from your incessant wrangling, from all this wasteful strife and enmity? Where were the peace and quiet that befitted your years, your profession, your station in life?[9]

7. Petrarch, "To Socrates," 135.
8. Petrarch, "To Marcus Tullius Cicero," 239.
9. Petrarch, "To Marcus Tullius Cicero," 240.

The letter continues with the details of the intrigues between Julius Caesar, Antony, and Octavian in which Cicero became tragically involved. Petrarch grieves that Cicero's end was one unbefitting a man of his caliber: "Ah! How much better it would have been, how much more fitting for a philosopher, to have grown old peacefully in the country, meditating, as you yourself have somewhere said, upon the life that endures forever."[10] It is as though Petrarch is genuinely grieving the tragedy that befell a close, intimate friend, one he feels free to admonish for his shortcomings. On the other hand, Petrarch closes his letter in a manner as if to emphasize the insurmountable distance between himself and his friend Cicero: "Written in the land of the living . . . on the 16th of June, and in the year of that God whom you never knew the 1345th."[11] While he and Cicero share a common love of letters and philosophy, the two remain separated on account of Cicero's death and his ignorance of Christ. It seems that, for Petrarch, even humanism is unable to transcend this distance between friends. While Renaissance humanism provides an exercise in imaginative friendship, it is unable to bridge the chronological and theological distance that separates Petrarch from his literary mentor.

In one of his letters to his contemporary Boccaccio (1313–1375), we see Petrarch's understanding of friendship most fully expressed. The two humanists enjoyed a close friendship based upon their shared love of Latin and Greek literature. At the same time, it was becoming fashionable for men-of-letters such as they to try their hands at writing prose and verse in the vernacular (in this case, Italian). In the letter, we read that Petrarch has recently learned of an action on the part of his friend Boccaccio: he burned his own early vernacular writings. Petrarch is distressed and puzzled by this, and writes the letter as a rebuke for such a rash act. In the opening paragraph, he sets the tone of the rebuke, that it is to be given—and hopefully, received—in the spirit of friendship: "Prepare your mind for patience and your ears for reproaches. For, although nothing could be more alike than our two minds, I

10. Petrarch, "To Marcus Tullius Cicero," 242.
11. Petrarch, "To Marcus Tullius Cicero," 242.

have often noticed with surprise that nothing could be more un-like than our acts and resolutions."[12] Petrarch and Boccaccio are of one mind in their love of literature, but this makes Boccaccio's action all the more incomprehensible. Why would he destroy his own writings? Petrarch speculates that Boccaccio was motivated by a sense of pride masking itself as humility. He had learned from one Donato, a mutual friend, that Boccaccio had recently read Petrarch's own Italian verse and, comparing his own unfavorably with Petrarch's, consigned his own verse to the flames. Petrarch writes:

> In this way you deprived both yourself and posterity of the fruits of your labours in this field of literature, and for no better reason than that you thought what you had written was inferior to my productions. But your dislike was ill-founded and the sacrifice inexpedient. As for your motive, that is doubtful. Was it humility, which despised itself, or pride, which would be second to none? You who can see your own heart must judge. I can only wander among the various possible conjectures, writing to you, as usual, as if I were talking to myself.[13]

While Boccaccio alone knows the real reason for the destruction of his own writings, Petrarch ventures to suggest false humility, the pride of refusing to be "second best." Yet there is no accusa-tion in this; Petrarch addresses Boccaccio as if he were addressing himself. He sees in his friend his other self, undoubtedly recogniz-ing in Boccaccio's action a temptation with which he himself has struggled. Still, Petrarch is grieved at this possible motive. Why is it such a disgraceful thing to be ranked next to Petrarch, he asks? Genuine friendship eschews all jealous rivalry: "True friends place those whom they love above themselves. They not only wish to be excelled, but experience an extreme pleasure in being outstripped, just as no fond father would deny that his greatest pleasure consist-ed in being surpassed by his son."[14] Furthermore, the affection of

12. Petrarch, "On the Italian Language," 197.
13. Petrarch, "On the Italian Language," 201.
14. Petrarch, "On the Italian Language," 205.

friendship renders the question of precedence irrelevant. Petrarch continues:

> He who sits in the chariot or runs by his friend's side does not ask who is first, but is only anxious that they two shall be as near as possible. Nothing is sweeter than the longed-for closeness of companionship. Love is everything, precedence next to nothing, among friends. The first are last and the last first, for all are truly one in friendship.[15]

There is thus an egalitarian quality to friendship, rendering both parties equal. True friendship is an antidote to pride. At the same time, this same friendship compels Petrarch to posit a higher and more respectable motive for Boccaccio's actions. Petrarch informs us that those who ventured into vernacular composition were often met with ridicule by self-styled, sophomoric literary critics. This led Boccaccio to destroy his own Italian compositions so as to protect them from such degrading criticism: "You did not destroy your productions, in a manner so unfair both to you and to them, through false pride, which is quite alien to your gentle character . . . You were actuated by a noble indignation against the emptiness and vanity of our age, which in its crass ignorance corrupts or, far worse, despises everything good."[16] Boccaccio's true motive was that of a conscientious humanist, and it is friendship, a genuine, intimate knowledge of Boccaccio's character, that enables Petrarch to recognize this.

Erasmus of Rotterdam

While Petrarch represents the stylistic and aesthetic preoccupations of the literary humanists of the Renaissance, Erasmus of Rotterdam (1466–1536) personifies what might be called a moralistic or reformist orientation. Erasmus is the most eminent figure in what is often called the "northern Renaissance." While humanists

15. Petrarch, "On the Italian Language," 206.
16. Petrarch, "On the Italian Language," 206.

throughout Europe were devoted to the works of classical antiquity, which served as the curricula for far-reaching educational reform, the humanists of northern Europe—i.e., France, the Netherlands, Germany, and England—paid particular attention to the writings of Christian antiquity, specifically the Bible and the fathers of the church. The early Christian patrimony, studied in its original languages and with due attention to historical context and literary genre, served as inspiration for the reform of the church and of Christian society. Erasmus stands out on account of the sheer immensity of his writings, his unmatched mastery of Greek and Latin, and the style and conviction with which he articulates his reformist vision, which is seen most fully in his *philosophia Christi*, the "philosophy of Christ." When examined in the context of this philosophy, friendship for Erasmus becomes the fundamental means of social reform.

We find the fullest exposition of the *philosophia Christi* in Erasmus's *Paraclesis*, the foreword to his Latin translation of the Greek New Testament. He laments the fact that Christians know less of this philosophy than the adherents of various philosophical schools know of their respective doctrines.[17] The teachings of these schools cannot make us happy, yet their adherents learn them by heart, while the teachings of Christ are barely known by Christians:

> Wouldn't anyone consider it shameful for a professed Aristotelian not to know the opinion of the master on the causes of lightning, the essence of matter, or infinity? These are matters that neither render us happy when we know them nor make us wretched when we don't. Yet we, brought to Christ through so many initiations, confirmed by so many sacraments, think it no shame or disgrace to be ignorant of his teachings which promise supreme happiness to all.[18]

What, then, characterizes the *philosophia Christi*? First, it is "a special mode of wisdom, so extraordinary that it renders foolish all

17. Erasmus, *Paraclesis*, 119–20.
18. Erasmus, *Paraclesis*, 119–20.

the wisdom of the world."[19] Second, it is constituted by the teachings of the New Testament, which is to be made accessible to all: "Christ wanted his mysteries to be disseminated as widely as possible . . . I would hope that the farmer might chant a holy text at his plow, the spinner sing it as she sits at her wheel, the traveler ease the tedium of his journey with tales from the scripture."[20] Third, it is a philosophy that transforms the entire person, taking root "in the human heart and in the total life of the individual."[21] Such a person, according to Erasmus, is a true "theologian," one who teaches "not by contorted syllogisms, but by his very demeanor and facial expression, by his eyes and tenor of his whole life."[22]

This *philosophia Christi*, for Erasmus, was the basis for comprehensive social reform. Were this philosophy implemented by rulers, taught in the classroom, and proclaimed from the pulpit, he maintains, the church and society would be transformed: "Christendom might not be convulsed by these all-but-endless wars, people might not be racked by such an insane fury to pile up riches any which way, sacred and profane business alike would not be torn up by such furious litigation."[23] The *philosophia Christi* is able to reform human society because it is a philosophy suitable to human nature: "Our philosophy sinks easily into the human mind because it is so largely in accord with human nature. What else is this philosophy of Christ, which he himself calls being born again, but renewal of a human nature originally well formed?"[24] Much of this same teaching, Erasmus argues, is found in the writings of the pagan philosophers.[25] "The Stoics," he writes, "recognized that no man was wise unless he was also good; they knew that nothing was truly good or honest except real virtue, nothing evil or shameful

19. Erasmus, *Paraclesis*, 119–20.

20. Erasmus, *Paraclesis*, 121.

21. Erasmus, *Paraclesis*, 123.

22. Erasmus, *Paraclesis*, 122.

23. Erasmus, *Paraclesis*, 122–23.

24. Erasmus, *Paraclesis*, 123–24.

25. Erasmus, *Paraclesis*, 123–24.

except dishonor alone."[26] Socrates taught "that an injury should not be repaid with an injury."[27] In Aristotle's *Politics*, we find "that nothing can be pleasant to us which is not in one degree or another degrading, with the solitary exception of virtue."[28] Erasmus thus brings classical thought into the service of his Christian humanism, ordering it to the teaching of Christ, who "taught his doctrine much more fully, and exemplified it even better."[29]

It is in the context of his *philosophia Christi* that the significance of Erasmus's conception of friendship becomes evident. We see this in his *Adagia*. The *Adagia* are a collection of adages or proverbs from various Greek and Latin classical authors, accompanied by essays in which Erasmus recounts the literary sources of the sayings and provides timely commentary on their significance.[30] The collecting of ancient proverbs fits well with the humanists' desire to recover the content and style of antiquity. Such a collection not only demonstrated the erudition of the compiler, but provided a ready resource for a reader desiring to become well-versed in the ancients. Adages were usually figurative, expressing commonplace ideas in metaphorical language, e.g., "Wine speaks the truth."[31] They also served a valuable pedagogical purpose, showing insight into perennial truths in a rhetorically attractive way. As Erasmus writes, "I think the best of them are those which equally give pleasure by their figurative colouring and profit by the value of their ideas."[32] To further vindicate the use of proverbs as opposed to a more rationalistic, prosaic approach, Erasmus cites their use in sacred Scripture: "Who would dare to despise this mode of speech, when he saw that some of the oracles of the holy

---

26. Erasmus, *Paraclesis*, 124.

27. Erasmus, *Paraclesis*, 123–24.

28. Erasmus, *Paraclesis*, 123–24.

29. Erasmus, *Paraclesis*, 123–24.

30. Olin, "Erasmus' *Adagia* and More's *Utopia*," 127.

31. Olin, "Erasmus' *Adagia* and More's *Utopia*," 6–7.

32. Erasmus, *Adages*, 13.

prophets are made of proverbs?"[33] Most importantly, Christ used this form of teaching:

> Who would not revere them as an almost holy thing, fit to express the mysteries of religion, since Christ Himself, whom we ought to imitate in all things, seems to have taken a particular delight in this way of speaking? An adage is current in Greek: "I judge the tree by its fruit." In Luke we read the same thing: "A good tree bringeth not forth corrupt fruit, neither doth a corrupt tree bring forth good fruit."[34]

From this it seems that adages play an indispensable role in Erasmus's *philosophia Christi*, wherein Christ, who is the supreme model for Christian conduct, provides Christian teachers and theologians with the most effective pedagogical method.

Several of Erasmus's adages have to do with friendship, e.g., "friendship is equality" (*amicitia aequalitas*) and "a friend is another self" (*amicus alter ipse*). In each case, he cites the adage and gives examples from antiquity. His most substantive adage, however, is the one with which he begins the collection: "friends have all things in common" (*amicorum communia omnia*).[35] He cites Socrates, Euripides, Terence, Cicero, Aristotle, and Plato as sources. We find in Plato, moreover, an indication of the role friendship plays in Erasmus's *philosophia Christi*. Erasmus writes:

> What else is Plato driving at in so many volumes save to promote community and its foundation, friendship? If he could convince mortals of these things, war, envy, fraud would immediately depart from our midst; in short a whole army of evils would march out of our lives once and for all.[36]

---

33. Erasmus, *Adages*, 13.

34. Erasmus, *Adages*, 13.

35. Olin, "Erasmus' *Adagia* and More's *Utopia*," 128.

36. Erasmus, *Adages*, 1.1.1, quoted in Olin, "Erasmus' *Adagia* and More's *Utopia*," 131.

Here, Erasmus suggests the importance of friendship in the reform of society, which is the chief aim of his Christian humanism. As seen in Erasmus's *Paraclesis*, classical writers bore witness to the same truths that were fully expounded and exemplified by Christ. This same adage, that friends possess all things in common, is found in Christianity. Here, however, it takes on a supernatural dimension:

> What other aim had Christ the prince of our religion? Truly He gave to the world only one precept, the rule of charity, and He stressed that everything in the Law and the Prophets hangs on that alone. Or, what else does charity urge save that all have all things in common? Namely, it urges that joined in friendship with Christ [*amicitia coagmentati cum Christo*] and bound to Him by the same force that unites Him with the Father and imitating as far as we can that perfect communion by which He and the Father are one we also become one with Him and, as Paul says, are made one spirit and one flesh in God, so that by right of friendship [*amicitiae iure*] all that is His is shared with us and all that is ours is shared with Him.[37]

Here, Erasmus equates friendship with charity. Friends have all things in common. Charity likewise joins people in a mutual sharing of goods. The root of this fellowship is the life of the Trinity, "that same force" uniting Christ with the Father. Thus, for Erasmus, the mystery of the intimate love between the Father and the Son not only transforms friendship, but it actually reveals its most profound meaning. Christian friendship, linking human beings in fellowship with each other and, through Christ, with the Father, thus becomes the basis for reforming Christian society by providing a trinitarian basis for social harmony. Moreover, this same charity-friendship brings not only human society, but also all creation, into a shared, cosmic fellowship: "Finally, charity urges that since the sum total of all created things is in God and God in turn

---

37. Erasmus, *Adages*, 1.1.1, quoted in Olin, "Erasmus' *Adagia* and More's *Utopia*," 131.

is in all things the whole universe is, as it were, [to] be restored to unity."[38]

Thomas More

We see the intense Christian humanist fellowship of friendship most fully exemplified in the friendship between Erasmus and Thomas More (1478–1535). More was every bit Erasmus's equal in scholarship, erudition, and commitment to church reform. More spent his early years deciding between a religious vocation and a desire to marry and pursue a legal career. He ultimately chose the latter, and very quickly rose to prominence in law and politics in London, becoming a judge and ultimately Lord Chancellor of England under Henry VIII. Erasmus and More first met when Erasmus visited More in England in 1499.[39] The two began an immediate and lifelong friendship rooted in common intellectual pursuits and a shared desire to rejuvenate the church through Christian humanism. In a letter written to Ulrich von Hutten, one of his many literary correspondents, Erasmus describes More as the very embodiment of the ideal of friendship. Hutten had read More's writings and had then written to Erasmus, desiring to know more about More's person. Erasmus informs Hutten that More had also read some of Hutten's writings, and was quite impressed, so much as to make Erasmus jealous.[40] Erasmus suggests that a friendship has already formed between More and Hutten on the basis of their mutual recognition of each other's intellectual abilities: "what Plato says of that sweetest wisdom, which excites much more ardent love among men than the most admirable beauty of form."[41] Erasmus sees in his friend Thomas More the Platonic ideal of love rooted, not in passing sensual pleasure, but in the abiding beauty of wisdom. He continues:

38. Erasmus, *Adages*, 1.1.1, quoted in Olin, "Erasmus' *Adagia* and More's *Utopia*," 131.

39. Sylvester, "More, Sir Thomas," 888.

40. Erasmus, "Letter to Ulrich von Hutten," 5–9.

41. Erasmus, "Letter to Ulrich von Hutten," 9–11.

and so it comes to pass that people are sometimes united in the warmest affection [*ardentissima caritate*] who have never seen or spoken to each other. And, as it is a common experience, that for some unexplained reason different people are attracted by different kinds of beauty, so between one mind and another, there seems to be a sort of latent kindred [*tacita cognatio*], which causes us to be specially delighted with some minds, and not with others.[42]

Thus More and Hutten enjoy *tacita cognatio*, a "latent kindred," or implicit friendship on the basis of their shared scholarly interests and like intellectual temperament. Erasmus then proceeds to give Hutten a lengthy character delineation of their mutual friend, "a friend, who is the most delightful character in the world."[43] After describing More's physical appearance, dietary habits, dress, and voice, Erasmus elucidates More's natural disposition for friendship: "He seems to be born and made for friendship, of which he is the sincerest and persistent devotee."[44] Erasmus continues:

When he has found any sincere friends, whose characters are suited to his own, he is so delighted with their society and conversation, that he seems to find in these the chief pleasure of life, having an absolute distaste for tennis and dice and cards, and the other games with which the mass of gentlemen beguile the tediousness of Time. It should be added that, while he is somewhat neglectful of his own interests, no one takes more pains in attending to the concerns of his friends. What more need I say? If anyone requires a perfect example of true friendship [*verae amicitiae exemplar*], it is in More that he will best find it.[45]

We notice here in Erasmus's description of More a crucial distinction between worldly pleasures and the pleasures of friendship. Thomas More is no bore; he takes hearty delight in the company

42. Erasmus, "Letter to Ulrich von Hutten," 13–17.

43. Erasmus, "Letter to Ulrich von Hutten," 20–21.

44. Erasmus, "Letter to Ulrich von Hutten," 87–88.

45. Erasmus, "Letter to Ulrich von Hutten," 93–99.

and conversation of good friends, but eschews tennis and gambling, the typical, refined pastimes of the upper class of which he is a member. Such activities, of course, involve human interaction, but they do not engage the person on the same level as intimate conversation. In amicable company there is an experience of interpersonal communion not found in mere diversion. In fact, More's company, his kindness and "sweetness of temper" are such that they "cheer the dullest spirit, and alleviate the annoyance of the most trying circumstances."[46] More's kindly disposition is able to provide merriment and cheer to all who are admitted to his company. Thus it is that More is *verae amicitiae exemplar*.

Erasmus also sees in his friend Thomas More one who personifies the refined sensibilities and affability characteristic of classical friendship. More has digested and now exemplifies the doctrine of friendship found in Plato, Aristotle, and Cicero. His true intimates are virtuous individuals who share his love of the things of the mind. At the same time, friendship takes on a more egalitarian quality for More not unlike that found in Petrarch but which, as we shall see, is more outward-looking and inclusive. More seems to have had a certain aversion to class distinctions and privileges, avoiding the company of the royal court and "having always [a] special hatred of tyranny and a great fancy for equality."[47] Thus, Erasmus tells us, More is not afraid to make "a multiplicity of friends," but is "accessible to every tender of intimacy" and is "by no means fastidious in choosing his acquaintance."[48] Beyond this, More's egalitarianism has a broader application. Having by this time assumed high office in the government, More is now in a position to help numerous people, both his close intimates as well as his amicable associates. More exhibits all of the social benefits that one expects from a friend, but extends them without distinction to anyone in need. Erasmus writes:

46. Erasmus, "Letter to Ulrich von Hutten," 100–101.

47. Erasmus, "Letter to Ulrich von Hutten," 79–80.

48. Erasmus, "Letter to Ulrich von Hutten," 89–90.

> It has always been part of his character to be most oblig-
> ing to everybody, and marvelously ready with his sympa-
> thy; and this disposition is more conspicuous than ever,
> now that his power of doing good is greater. Some he
> relieves with money, some he protects by his authority,
> some he promotes by his recommendation, while those
> whom he cannot otherwise assist are benefited by his ad-
> vice. No one is sent away in distress, and you might call
> him the general patron of all poor people. He counts it a
> great gain to himself, if he has relieved some oppressed
> person, made the path clear for one that was in difficul-
> ties, or brought back into favor one that was in disgrace.
> No man more readily confers a benefit, no man expects
> less in return.[49]

We notice again the idea of the friend as another self: he "counts it
a great gain to himself" to assist someone in distress. More, however, does not limit this aspect of friendship to his close friends,
but to all who need his assistance. His solicitude for the poor was
such that he came to be called "the best friend that the poor e'er
had."[50] More's egalitarianism is a natural outgrowth of Christian
charity.

Not only did More's friendship include those with whom he
did not enjoy close personal relationships; it extended even to his
enemies. This is rooted in what James McEvoy has aptly called
More's "eschatological ideal of friendship."[51] Not only is friendship on earth continued in heaven, but the hope of the fellowship
of heaven enables one to regard one's earthly enemies as one's
friends. As Lord Chancellor of England, More came to be caught
in the middle of the conflict between King Henry VIII and Pope
Clement VII over Henry's obsessive desire to nullify his marriage
to Catherine of Aragon so as to marry his mistress, Anne Boleyn.
After all of his diplomatic efforts had failed, Henry induced the
English Parliament, with the consent of almost all of the English
bishops, to sever the connection between the church in England

49. Erasmus, "Letter to Ulrich von Hutten," 219–27.

50. Shakespeare, "Book of Sir Thomas More," 1.14.44.

51. McEvoy, "Theory of Friendship," 243.

and the papacy. Parliament and the bishops declared the king and his successors "the only supreme head in earth of the Church of England."[52] In order to strengthen the Act of Supremacy, an oath was administered in which the oath-taker acknowledged the king's supremacy over the English church. Thomas More refused to take the oath, was imprisoned, and eventually convicted of high treason, for which the penalty was death.[53] At his condemnation, standing before his judges, he had this to say:

> More have I not to say, my lords, but that like the blessed apostle St. Paul, as we read in the Acts of the Apostles, was present, and consented to the death of St. Stephen, and kept their clothes that stoned him to death, and yet be they now both twain holy saints in heaven, and shall continue there friends forever, so I verily trust, and shall therefore right heartily pray, that though your lordships have now here in earth been judges to my condemnation, we may yet hereafter in heaven merrily all meet together, to our everlasting salvation.[54]

We notice that More goes beyond the Christian obligation to forgive those who have unjustly condemned him. His charity goes to the point of including them in the hope of friendship in the life to come. Thus, Thomas More personifies the doctrine of Thomas Aquinas, that friendship is perfected in charity and ordered toward universality. The final phrase is particularly striking: "we may yet hereafter in heaven merrily all meet to together." More hopes for something bigger than reconciliation between himself and his persecutors. He desires to enjoy with them all of the fellowship and conviviality that characterize friendship. This sentiment is reflected in the closing line of a meditation he composed while in the Tower of London, awaiting his execution: "To think my greatest enemies my best friends; for the brethren of Joseph could never have done him so much good with their love and favor as they

---

52. "Act of Supremacy (1534)."
53. Sylvester, "More, Sir Thomas," 890.
54. Roper, *Life of Sir Thomas More*, 54–55.

did him with their malice and hatred."[55] Christian friendship, for Thomas More, is able to reorder even the ill-will of one's enemies toward interpersonal communion.

Conclusion

The theme of friendship enjoys a prominent place in the writings of Renaissance humanists. Petrarch, Erasmus, and Thomas More shared a common love for the life of the mind and the refinement of intellectual and literary tastes that defined humanism. In addition, they were keenly aware of the interpersonal and moral dimensions of friendship. In Petrarch's correspondence, we see the abiding importance of interpersonal communion, both with his contemporary Boccaccio and even with the writers of antiquity, especially Cicero. His friendship with one long dead suggests the ability of friendship to transcend the limits of time and place, although their differences in religious belief (specifically Cicero's ignorance of Christ) make this transcendence problematic. His letter to his contemporary Boccaccio emphasizes the egalitarian quality of friendship, rendering friends equal and serving as an antidote to that pride which tempts us to value precedence and achievement, even at the expense of others. In Erasmus, we see friendship as a means of social reform, serving as it does the heart of his *philosophia Christi*. Genuine friendship unites all people in the very same charity shared between God the Father and God the Son, thus providing a solid, unassailable basis for Christian society, banning all conflict, strife and even war. Erasmus also reveals to us the personification of friendship in his friend Thomas More, who for the sake of friendship personally provided assistance, and even merriment, to all who came to him. In addition, like Petrarch, More recognized not only a certain egalitarian quality in friendship, but also understood genuine friendship to transcend time. A key difference between the two, however, is the role played by Christian faith. For Petrarch, faith underscored the chasm between

55. More, "Meditation on Detachment," 150.

himself and his ancient friend Cicero. For Thomas More, faith served as the very basis of a time-transcending friendship, looking forward to the unending communion of persons he would enjoy with his friends in heaven, even with those whom on earth he had regarded as his enemies. Thus, in the Renaissance, we have three Christian humanist thinkers whose literary sensibilities exhibit an ongoing, even heightened, awareness of the wider social implications of friendship.

5

Toward a Culture of Friendship: Some Personal Reflections

IN THE INTRODUCTION, I stated that friendship is the apogee of culture, that it gives culture its vital importance, and that because of this, transforming the culture is also of vital importance: it is an essential part of the mission of the church. What, then, is the relationship between friendship and the transformation of culture? We defined culture as the collection of values, beliefs, and customs of a society along with its artistic, intellectual, and social achievements, and as the cultivation of human nature, enabling us to live in communion with others. What role does Christian friendship play in the transformation of culture thus understood? Since Christian friendship is both the basis and the expression of the integration of faith and life, by cultivating genuine Christian friendship, we take the greatest interpersonal achievement of culture and reorient it to participation in God's own triune life.

What is the cultural good that we call friendship? From classical antiquity, we learn that friendship is rooted in virtue; that it involves the pursuit of wisdom; that it seeks the good of the friend, even to the point of dying for the friend; that it regards the friend as another self; that it is ordered to the good of the community; and that it continues even after death via *memoria*. This is the cultural heritage bequeathed to us by classical antiquity, the values that the classical tradition of friendship has given to us. All of these qualities were taken up and transformed by the Catholic tradition. For Christian thinkers, friendship is rooted in and fulfilled in Christ. It is now ordered to the contemplation of that true wisdom that became incarnate. It sees in Christ the true pattern of self-sacrificial dying for one's friend. It regards the friend as another self to such an extent that to betray the friend is to betray Christ. It is ordered to the good of the community in terms of providing the impetus of the reform of society according to the teachings of Christ. It takes on an expansive and inclusive dimension, loving the friend "in God" and the enemy "for the sake of God." Finally, it is ordered toward the communion of saints, which gives friendship a perpetuity that goes beyond classical *memoria*.

The transformation of culture, however, requires more than merely taking up and transforming the values of antiquity. There is a deep-seated disorder in our culture in regard to human relationships, a disorder that presents a grave threat to human dignity. We remember that human dignity is rooted in relationality, which is at the heart of our being made in God's image and likeness. We possess self-knowledge, self-possession, the ability to enter into communion with others, and are called to enter a covenant relationship with God. It was the violation of this covenant by our first parents that introduced sin into the world, and which introduced disorder into our relationships. Our self-knowledge is darkened and distorted. Our self-possession is likewise wounded, and consequently so is our ability to enter into meaningful relationships with other persons.

There is much in our contemporary culture that evinces this distortion of human relationships. Pope Francis has devoted considerable attention to what he calls a "throw-away culture" that treats the goods of creation with a contempt rooted in undisciplined consumption and consumerism: "Human beings" he writes, "are themselves considered consumer goods to be used and then discarded. We have created a 'throw away' culture which is now spreading."[1] John Paul II earlier recognized this tendency in a contemporary society that had lost its sense of God's presence:

1. Francis, *Evangelii Gaudium*, 1.53.

> The values of being are replaced by those of having. The only goal which counts is the pursuit of one's own material well-being. The so-called "quality of life" is interpreted primarily or exclusively as economic efficiency, inordinate consumerism, physical beauty and pleasure, to the neglect of the more profound dimensions—interpersonal, spiritual and religious—of existence.[2]

Consumerism is inherently anti-relational. It reduces all created goods to objects to be exploited for pleasure or efficiency. It also fosters a sense of isolation and even desperation, in which other persons are seen as mortal competitors for such goods, and since the human person is also a created good, this reductionist tendency sooner or later subjects the person to such exploitation. The "values of having" cultivate a self-centeredness, even a certain viciousness, that not only destroys relationships but also destroys persons.

The reduction of the human person to pleasure or efficiency takes many different forms, all of which are interconnected. The most poignant expression of this is in human sexuality. Nowhere does our breach of the covenant relationship with our Creator reveal itself more forcefully than here. Having violated our relationship with God, our intellect has become darkened. This, in turn, skews our ability to understand our Creator's plan for human sexuality, its nature and its orientation toward genuine happiness. We see this in many areas, but particularly in three phenomena: pornography, the breakdown of marriage, and homosexuality. Pornography addiction is one of the most personally, socially, and spiritually destructive problems besetting our society. It creates in the addict not only a wholly unrealistic expectation in regard to sex, but also makes the addict self-absorbed to the point of being unable to make a genuine act of self-giving or receive the self-gift of another. Thus, it undermines the ability of spouses to give themselves fully to each other in the conjugal act, and since the conjugal act is one of the most powerful ways in which the nuptial bond is strengthened, this undermining weakens the marriage itself.

2. John Paul II, *Evangelium Vitae*, 1.23.

Furthermore, since all relationships, including non-sexual ones, involve some level of self-donation and reception, this deep-seated self-absorption undermines every facet of the person's interaction with others. Thus, while this crippling of self-donation destroys the intimacy of marriage, it also destroys non-spousal intimacy as well. A porn-addict is clearly incapable of being a faithful spouse, but is such a person even capable of being a genuine friend?

Homosexuality is a very heated topic; it is also very sensitive, and must be addressed with a commitment to the truth as well as compassion. While the cause of the homosexual orientation remains a matter of debate, Christian morality cannot condone homosexual behavior, seeing how that behavior not only violates the procreative dimensions of the sexual act, but also does not proceed from the natural complementarity between the sexes.[3] One of the effects of the sexual revolution, however, has been contempt for this male-female complementarity. This emerges, I believe, from two attitudes. First, sex is seen in radically individualistic terms, i.e., ordered primarily if not entirely to a subjective sense of self-fulfillment. Second, our culture has idolized sexual pleasure. Thus, sex has now become a new "secular religion."[4] Religion, by its nature, entails a holistic view of life. If sex is one's religion, then everything in one's life is "sexualized." Thus, the very idea of non-sexual intimacy becomes incomprehensible to many people. At the same time, the desire for interpersonal intimacy found within any relationship is genuine and good. Perhaps a recovery of friendship is the genuine, compassionate, and truth-ordered response to the struggles of homosexual persons. The classical tradition teaches us that friendship is the highest form of human intimacy; it is chaste, nonsexual, and the most humanizing of human pleasures. The Christian tradition affirms this, and takes it a step further: friendship is the means of ascent to God.

Perhaps the most tragic form the reduction of the person takes, one that results as a matter of course from our distortion of human sexuality, is abortion. In the United States, the abortion

3. *Catechism of the Catholic Church*, para. 2357.
4. Eberstadt, "Zealous Faith of Secularism."

issue is the epicenter of the culture war. No other single issue is able to evoke such indignation, and this on both sides of the controversy. Not only does abortion involve the taking of an innocent human life, but the life is taken in the name of a supposedly constitutional right, the so-called "right to choose." The abortion license is understood to be protected under the category of a so-called "right to privacy," and while no reasonable person would deny that there is a basic and implicit right to privacy within a free society, it is disturbing, to say the least, that this right is understood to include the right to take the life of an unborn child. I am convinced that this right to privacy, when used as a justification for abortion, expresses a profound interpersonal alienation. This alienation is obviously felt between the expectant mother and her unborn child, who is now regarded as an "enemy," a status resulting from the hedonistic view of sex that is at the root of the "contraceptive mentality" so prevalent in our society. John Paul II writes that abortion and contraception both stem from "a hedonistic mentality" that is unwilling to accept basic responsibility in regard to sex:

> They imply a self-centered concept of freedom, which regards procreation as an obstacle to personal fulfilment. The life which could result from a sexual encounter thus becomes an enemy to be avoided at all costs, and abortion becomes the only possible decisive response to failed contraception.[5]

I would add that, in addition to the hedonistic view of sex, there is another factor that causes the unborn child to be regarded as an enemy. That factor is fear born from alienation between the mother and those closest to her, i.e., the father of the child, her family. Thus there is a twofold alienation: between the mother and her unborn child, and between the mother and those in her life. Those to whom the mother should be able to turn for support often abandon her or threaten her with abandonment unless she has an abortion.

---

5. John Paul II, *Evangelium Vitae*, 1.13.

We also see this same anti-relational dynamic at work in the practice of euthanasia. There is a profound sense of loneliness behind a request for medically assisted suicide, one in which the terminally-ill person's sense of self-worth, derived in no small measure from human relationship, has been lost. Again, John Paul II expresses the relational root of the crisis very well:

> When earthly existence draws to a close, it is again char-
> ity which finds the most appropriate means for enabling
> the elderly, especially those who can no longer look after
> themselves, and the terminally ill to enjoy genuinely
> humane assistance and to receive an adequate response
> to their needs, in particular their anxiety and their
> loneliness.[6]

In both abortion and euthanasia, the right to privacy becomes an expression, not of a healthy proper self-determination, but of a profound breakdown of human relationship. Christian charity, of course, summons us to accompany those in these seemingly hopeless situations. Friendship, specifically the dimension in which the suffering person experiences the empathy of a friend who has become "another self," can overcome the alienation and fear that lead to abortion and euthanasia.

What all of these tragedies share is a fundamental confusion as to the nature of the human person. The human person is relational in nature. Most people would not disagree with this, and would recognize that we are "social animals." Christianity and secularism disagree about the basis of this relationality. Either it is rooted in a transcendent, religious reality, or it is not. If it is, then human relationships serve a transcendent end. They are ordered to the person's life with God. If not, then relationships ultimately serve whatever purpose we choose to give them. These can be as altruistic as the survival of the species and/or society, or as ego-centric as personal fulfillment and physical pleasure. In such a view, the human person has no intrinsic value, and any attempt to forge friendship within this context will be self-defeating. Sooner

6. John Paul II, *Evangelium Vitae*, 4.88.

CHRISTIAN FRIENDSHIP

or later, it will degenerate into friendship of pleasure or utility, which both classical and Christian thinkers recognize as false friendships. Such friendships merely reinforce self-alienation and interpersonal alienation. If, however, human relationality is rooted in the nature of God, then it is ordered toward a mutual thriving rooted in self-giving love. Human friendship, understood within a Christian context, orders human relationships to this self-giving love. The goods of friendship, which are the highest achievements of culture, reach their true fulfillment, and thus contribute to the recovery and restoration of one's relationship with self—i.e., self-knowledge and self-possession—as well as one's communion with others.

Sadly, our culture seems to be dominated by an impoverished understanding of human relationality. Such a culture clearly needs to be healed and transformed at the root. Culture is transformed when taken up and reordered to its transcendent goal in Christ. We need to reorder human relationships to their supernatural end. Christian friendship, I believe, is the way of achieving this. How can this reordering be achieved in a culture that experiences such profound alienation between persons? How can Christian friendship bring healing and transformation to our culture? Perhaps what the church needs at this point is to build a "culture of friendship." Drawing again upon the Latin *cultus*, a culture of friendship would "cultivate" the goods of friendship so as to create a genuinely humane community, one in which human beings live and behave as authentic persons created in the image of God. What would such a culture look like? It would be constituted by interpersonal relationships that produce the goods of friendship. The first of these is a shared commitment to virtue, which includes the natural, supernatural, and theological virtues. The natural virtues—i.e., prudence, justice, fortitude, and temperance—are rooted in our natural human capacities and are ordered toward happiness in this life. When these same virtues are infused with divine grace, they are elevated to the supernatural order and thus prepare us to enjoy eternal life.[7] The theological virtues, in turn, include faith,

7. Groeschel, *Virtue Driven Life*, 20.

hope, and charity, and are not merely "elevated" natural virtues, but derive their origin directly from God, who infuses them into the soul at baptism and without which a person cannot be saved. While the theological virtues aim directly at eternal life, still they vivify temporal life and provide the proper *ultima* or goal of all social life: life with God. They also remind us that true friendship, in the words of Aelred, begins "in Christ," is "maintained according to Christ," and is finally "referred to Christ."[8] It is thus in light of the theological virtues that the eternal importance and significance of friendship is discerned. A recovery of friendship's eternal significance would serve as a reminder that all human relationships derive their ultimate meaning from our covenant with God, and therefore must be ordered according to God's plan.

A culture of friendship would also be characterized by a commitment to the common good, by common action for the good of the community. An awareness of the needs of one's neighbor and a common commitment to ensuring that those needs are met are powerful ways of fostering a coherent understanding of the common good, even if this understanding never becomes formally articulated. We move toward this understanding of the needs of the other by viewing the other in the light of friendship. The illuminative power of friendship shows us what is necessary for human thriving and promotes further reflection on friendship in its philosophical and theological dimensions. In addition, such a culture would include genuine empathy; that is, viewing the friend as another self. Such empathy—and this is perhaps the most challenging aspect—would need to extend to all, both inside and outside the church, and must particularly include those with whom one has pronounced ideological differences. Debate concerning fundamental areas of social, moral, and political disagreement would then be undertaken with a mutual presumption of good will. Finally, a culture of friendship would be constantly mindful, either explicitly or implicitly, of what Thomas More recognized: the eschatological communion of persons, to which all human beings are called and to which friendship points us.

8. Aelred, *Spiritual Friendship*, 1.8.

Bibliography

"The Act of Supremacy (1534)." http://tudorhistory.org/primary/supremacy. html.

Aelred of Rievaulx. *Spiritual Friendship*. Translated by Lawrence C. Braceland. Kalamazoo, MI: Cistercian, 2010.

Ambrose. *De Officiis*. Translated by Ivor J. Davidson. Oxford: Oxford University Press, 2001.

Anselm. *The Letters of Saint Anselm of Canterbury, Volume One*. Translated by Walter F. Fröhlich. Kalamazoo, MI: Cistercian, 1990.

Aristotle. *De Anima*. Edited by Richard McKeon. New York: Random House, 1941.

———. *Nicomachean Ethics*. Translated by Terence Irwin. Indianapolis: Hackett, 1985.

Augustine. *Confessions*. Translated by Henry Chadwick. Oxford: Oxford University Press, 1998.

Baltzly, Dirk, and Nick Eliopolous. "The Classical Ideals of Friendship." In *Friendship: A History*, edited by Barbara Caine, 1–64. Oxford: Routledge, 2014.

Benedict of Nursia. *Rule for Monasteries*. Translated by Leonard J. Doyle. Collegeville: Liturgical, 1948.

Benedict XVI. *Deus Caritas Est*. Washington, DC: United States Conference of Catholic Bishops, 2006.

———. *Holy Mass for the New Evangelization*. http://w2.vatican.va/content/ benedict-xvi/en/homilies/2011/documents/hf_ben-xvi_hom_20111016_ nuova-evang.html.

———. *Homily of His Holiness Benedict XVI*. http://w2.vatican.va/content/ benedict-xvi/en/homilies/2011/documents/hf_ben-xvi_hom_20111016_ nuova-evang.html.

———. "Wounded by the Arrow of Beauty: The Cross and New 'Aesthetics' of Faith." In *On the Way to Jesus Christ*, edited by Joseph Cardinal Ratzinger and translated by Michael J. Miller, 32–41. San Francisco: Ignatius, 2005.

Böckmann, Aquinata. "Approaching Christ in the Rule of Benedict." *Cistercian Studies Quarterly* 44.1 (2009) 21–38.

Caine, Barbara, ed. *Friendship: A History*. Oxford: Routledge, 2014.

Cassian, John. *Conferences*. http://www.newadvent.org/fathers/3508.htm.

Catechism of the Catholic Church. New York: Doubleday, 1995.

Catholic Study Bible: Revised Standard Version. Catholic Edition. San Francisco: Ignatius, 2006.

Chiovaro, F. "Cassian, John." In *The New Catholic Encyclopedia* 3:205–7.

Cicero, Marcus Tullius. *De Amicitia*. Translated by William Armistead Falconer. Cambridge: Harvard University Press, 1992.

———. *De Oratore*. Translated by Harris Rackham and E. W. Sutton. Cambridge: Harvard University Press, 1992.

Copleston, Frederick C. *A History of Medieval Philosophy*. Notre Dame: University of Notre Dame Press, 1972.

Eberstadt, Mary. "The Zealous Faith of Secularism: How the Sexual Revolution Became a Dogma." *First Things* 279 (2008) 35–40.

Erasmus, Desiderius. *Collected Works of Erasmus: Adages Ii1 to Iv100*. Notes by R. A. B. Mynors and translated by Margaret Mann Phillips. Toronto: University of Toronto Press, 1982.

———. "Letter to Ulrich von Hutten." https://www.thomasmorestudies.org/docs/Erasmus%20to%20Ulrich%20von%20Hutten.pdf

———. *Paraclesis: The Praise of Folly and Other Writings*. Edited and translated by Robert M. Adams. New York: Norton, 1989.

Francis, Pope. *Evangelii Gaudium*. Vatican City: Libreria Edictrice Vaticana, 2013.

Gregory the Great. *Forty Gospel Homilies*. Translated by Dom David Hurst. Kalamazoo, MI: Cistercian, 1990.

Gregory of Nazianzus. *Funeral Oration on St. Basil the Great: Funeral Orations by Saint Gregory Nazienzen and Saint Ambrose*. Translated by Leo P. McCauley et al. Washington, DC: Catholic University of America Press, 2004.

Groeschel, Benedict. *The Virtue Driven Life*. Huntington: Our Sunday Visitor, 2006.

Groeschel, Benedict, and Kevin Perrotta. *The Journey Toward God: In the Footsteps of the Great Spiritual Writers, Catholic, Protestant and Orthodox*. Cincinnati: Servant, 2000.

Haraguchi, Takaaki. "*Philia* as *Agape*: The Theme of Friendship in the Gospel of John." *Asia Journal of Theology* 28.2 (2014) 250–62.

John Paul II. *Christifideles Laici*. http://w2.vatican.va/content/john-paul-ii/en/apost_exhortations/documents/hf_jp-ii_exh_30121988_christifideles-laici.html.

———. *Evangelium Vitae*. http://w2.vatican.va/content/john-paul-ii/en/encyclicals/documents/hf_jp-ii_enc_25031995_evangelium-vitae.html.

———. *Salvifici Doloris*. http://w2.vatican.va/content/john-paul-ii/en/apost_letters/1984/documents/hf_jp-ii_apl_11021984_salvifici-doloris.html.

Kardong, Terrence. *Benedict's Rule: A Translation and Commentary*. Collegeville: Liturgical, 1996.

Kreeft, Peter. *Catholic Christianity: A Complete Catechism of Catholic Beliefs based on the* Catechism of the Catholic Church. San Francisco: Ignatius, 2001.

———. *How to Win the Culture War.* Downer's Grove, IL: InterVarsity, 2002.

Kroeber, A. L., and Clyde Kluckhohn. *Culture: A Critical Review of Concepts and Definitions.* Westport, CT: Greenwood, 1985.

Lang, O. "Culture." In *The New Catholic Encyclopedia* 4:426–36.

Lawrence, C. H. *Medieval Monasticism: Forms of Religious Life in Western Europe and the Middle Ages.* 3rd ed. Harlow, UK: Pearson Education, 2001.

Leclercq, Jean. *The Love of Learning and the Desire for God: A Study of Monastic Culture.* New York: Fordham University Press, 1982.

Lysias. "For the Soldier." In *Lysias*, translated by S. C. Todd, 95–100. Oratory of Classical Greece Series. Austin: University of Texas Press, 2000.

McEvoy, James. "The Theory of Friendship in Erasmus and Thomas More." *American Catholic Philosophical Quarterly* 80.2 (2006) 227–52.

McGuire, Brian Patrick. *Friendship and Community: The Monastic Experience, 350–1250.* Ithaca: Cornell University Press, 2010.

McGuire, M. R. P. "Ambrose, St." In *The New Catholic Encyclopedia* 1:337–40.

More, Thomas. "A Meditation on Detachment." In *The Sadness of Christ and Final Prayers and Benedictions*, edited by Gerard Wegemer and translated by Clarence Miller, 148–50. Princeton, NJ: Scepter, 1993.

Nawar, Tamer. "*Adiutrix Virtutum?* Augustine on Friendship and Virtue." In *Ancient and Medieval Concepts of Friendship*, edited by Suzanne Stern-Gillet and Gary M. Gurtler, 197–226. New York: State University of New York Press, 2014.

Niebuhr, H. Richard. *Christ and Culture.* New York: Harper & Row, 1951.

Olin, John C. "Erasmus' *Adagia* and More's *Utopia*." In *Miscellanea Moreana: Essays for Germain Marc'hadour*, edited by Clare M. Murphy et al., 127–36. Medieval & Renaissance Texts & Studies Series 61. Binghamton: Medieval & Renaissance Texts & Studies, 1989.

Petrarch, Francesco. "On the Italian Language and Literature to Boccaccio." In *Petrarch: The First Modern Scholar and Man of Letters*, edited by James Harvey Robinson, 197–214. New York: Putnam, 1898. https://history.hanover.edu/texts/petrarch/peto7.html.

———. "To Marcus Tullius Cicero." In *Petrarch: The First Modern Scholar and Man of Letters*, edited by James Harvey Robinson, 239–42. New York: Putnam, 1898. Hanover College History Department. https://history.hanover.edu/texts/petrarch/peto9.html.

———. "To Socrates." In *Petrarch: The First Modern Scholar and Man of Letters*, edited by James Harvey Robinson, 130–51. New York: Putnam, 1898. https://history.hanover.edu/texts/petrarch/peto2.html.

Pieper, Josef. *Leisure: the Basis of Culture.* South Bend: St. Augustine's, 1998.

Pincombe, Michael. *Elizabethan Humanism: Literature and Learning in the Later Sixteenth Century.* London: Routledge, 2013.

Plato. *Phaedrus*. In *Plato: Complete Works*, edited by John M. Cooper Jr. and D. S. Hutchinson, 506–56. Indianapolis: Hackett, 1997.

———. *Republic*. In *Plato: Complete Works*, edited by John M. Cooper Jr. and D. S. Hutchinson, 971–1223. Indianapolis: Hackett, 1997.

Ratzinger, Joseph Cardinal. *The New Evangelization: Building the Civilization of Love*. http://www.ewtn.com/new_evangelization/Ratzinger.htm.

Reeve, C. D. C. "Plato on Friendship and Eros." http://plato.stanford.edu/archives/sum2016/entries/plato-friendship.

Robertson, Duncan. *Lectio Divina: The Medieval Experience of Reading*. Collegeville: Cistercian, 2011.

Robson, Stephen. *"With the Spirit and Power of Elijah" (Lk 1,17): The Prophetic-Reforming Spirituality of Bernard of Clairvaux as Evidenced Particularly in His Letters*. Rome: Edictrice Pontificia Università Gregoriana, 2004.

Roper, William. *The Life of Sir Thomas More, c. 1556*. Edited by Gerard B. Wegemer and Stephen W. Smith. Irving, TX: Center for Thomas More Studies, 2003. https://thomasmorestudies.org/docs/Roper.pdf.

Shakespeare, William. "The Book of Sir Thomas More." In *The Oxford Shakespeare: The Complete Works*, edited by Stanley Wells and Gary Taylor, 813–42. 2nd ed. Oxford: Clarendon, 2005.

Southern, Richard W. *Saint Anselm: A Portrait in a Landscape*. Cambridge: Cambridge University Press, 1990.

Sylvester, R. S. "More, Sir Thomas." In *The New Catholic Encyclopedia* 9:887–93.

Thomas Aquinas. *Summa Theologiae*. 2nd and rev. ed. Translated by Fathers of the English Dominican Province. N.p.: Knight, 1920. http://www.newadvent.org/summa/.

Vergerius, Petrus Paulus. "De Ingenuis Moribus" ["On Noble Manners"]. In *Vittorino da Feltre and other Humanist Educators*, edited by W. H. Woodward, 93–118. Cambridge: Cambridge University Press, 1912. https://history.hanover.edu/texts/verg.html.

Name/Subject Index

Scripture Index